EVERYTHING HORSE FOR BEGINNERS

HOW A HORSE'S BRAIN WORKS AND OTHER FUNDAMENTAL EQUINE INFORMATION

LM TAYLOR

CONTENTS

INTRODUCTION

THE HORSE

 Where in this wide world can man find nobility without pride, friendship without envy or beauty without vanity? Here, where grace is laced with muscle, and strength by gentleness confined. He serves without servility; he has fought without enmity. There is nothing so powerful, nothing less violent, there is nothing so quick, nothing more patient.

— RONALD DUNCAN

Have you ever looked into a horse's deep, soulful eyes and felt an inexplicable connection? Or watched in awe as a majestic equine gracefully gallops across an open field? Horses are not just animals; they are powerful, intelligent creatures that have captured our hearts and imaginations for centuries. Whether you're an experienced equestrian or simply admire these beautiful animals from afar, there's no denying that horses are truly fascinating creatures.

For centuries, horses have been more than just animals to humans—they have been sources of inspiration, companions, and even symbols of power and nobility. The intricate relationship between humans and horses is evident in art, culture, and history, where these majestic creatures have been depicted in a multitude of forms.

From ancient times to the modern era, horses have been represented in countless works of art, including paintings, sculptures, and even tapestries. Their grace, beauty, and power have been captured in some of the most iconic artworks of all time, from the Parthenon frieze in ancient Greece to the Renaissance masterpieces of Leonardo da Vinci and Michelangelo.

But horses are more than just a subject of art—they have also played a crucial role in human history, from transportation to warfare. Horses have been used for transportation for centuries, carrying people and goods long distances. They were also an essential part of many armies, providing swift and powerful cavalry charges that could turn the tide of battle.

In many cultures, horses have become symbols of power, nobility, and even divinity. In ancient Greece, for example, the winged horse Pegasus was believed to be a messenger of the gods. Horses were associated with chivalry and the knightly code of honor in medieval Europe.

Even today, horses continue to captivate us with their beauty and majesty. From horse racing to show jumping, from carriage rides to trail rides, there are countless ways that humans and horses interact and connect. So if you've ever been entranced by the sight of a galloping horse or felt a sense of awe in their presence, you're not alone - horses have been captivating humans for centuries, and they will continue to do so for generations to come.

GALLOPING THROUGH TIME

> *Wherever man has left his footprint in the long ascent from barbarism to civilization we will find the hoofprint of the horse beside it.*

— *JOHN MOORE*

We are here to talk about horses. These majestic creatures have been by our side for centuries, carrying us through wars, plowing our fields, and even helping us explore the vastness of space.

But have you ever wondered about the evolutionary history of horses? How did these incredible animals come to be the graceful creatures we know and love today? Well, fear not, for that is precisely what we will explore in this chapter. We will delve deep into the genetic makeup and adaptations that have helped horses survive and thrive throughout the ages.

So sit back, grab a carrot (or an apple), and travel through time and space to explore the fascinating world of horses.

EVOLUTION OF HORSES

The evolution of horses can be traced back to over 50 million years ago when they were small, dog-sized creatures known as Eohippus or "dawn horse." These early horses lived in dense forests and had four toes on their front feet and three toes on their back feet. Over time, their bodies and feet evolved to adapt to changing environments, and the modern horse eventually emerged.

One of the most significant adaptations of horses was the development of a single, strong hoof on each foot. This adaptation allowed horses to run faster and with more stability, making them better able to escape predators in open grasslands. In addition, their teeth evolved to become larger and flatter, enabling them to graze on tougher grasses.

As horses evolved, they grew taller and larger, with longer legs and more powerful muscles. They also developed a highly efficient digestive system to extract maximum nutrients from grass and other plant materials. These adaptations made them better suited for running long distances, which was essential for survival in the wild.

Another key factor in the evolution of horses was their relationship with humans. Humans domesticated horses around 4000 BCE, developing different breeds for specific purposes, such as racing, riding, or pulling heavy loads. Today, there are over 350 breeds of horses worldwide, each with a unique set of characteristics and traits.

EQUINE BEHAVIOR: PREY VS. PREDATOR

As you delve into the world of horses, it's important to understand that these majestic creatures don't reason whether an animal is a predator or not. Horses have evolved to take flight first and think later, relying on their instincts for survival. This means that horses can be scared of animals that are not predators, such as mules, donkeys, goats, cows, and even other horses pulling carts. Or, as any horseman will tell you, horses are frequently scared of almost anything and everything, especially when they first encounter it.

A story that perfectly illustrates this is that of a stock horse named Little Digger. Despite being an experienced competitor in shows and camp drafts, Little Digger would still freak out and bolt around his paddock when he saw a horse and cart coming up the road for no apparent reason.

It's important to remember that when humans first approach young horses, they can be as frightened as if a cougar were approaching them. When in doubt, horses don't take the time to reason which animals (and sometimes inanimate objects) are predators and which aren't; they rely solely on their instincts. So, as you spend time around horses, it's crucial to be aware of their natural tendencies as a prey animal and approach them with care and patience.

Vision

As prey animals, horses have evolved to have exceptional vision, which has become vital to their survival strategy. Let's dive deeper into how horses have adapted their vision to stay alive in the wild.

Panoramic Field View and Acuity

Firstly, horses have a unique panoramic field of view, meaning they can see almost everything around them without moving their head. Their eyes are on the sides of their head, allowing them to see nearly 360 degrees around them. This ability is critical in the wild as it enables horses to spot predators approaching from any direction, even behind. However, due to their wide-set eyes, horses have a blind spot directly in front of their face, so they tend to lower their heads when examining an object closely.

Additionally, horses have exceptional visual acuity, meaning they can see fine details and distinguish between colors. This ability helps them to identify potential food sources and spot any danger from a distance. Therefore, horses can recognize their owners or other horses from far away and see predators or other threats from a distance.

For example, one of my bedroom windows faces my main pasture. I usually get up and look out that window first thing in the morning. If my horses are in that pasture, they always notice the movement in the window and turn and look in my direction. That field is three to four football fields away from my house, but even from that distance and inside the house behind the glass, they still see me and react every single time, even it's just a raise of the head.

Night Vision and Color Vision

Another critical aspect of horses' vision is their ability to see in low-light conditions. Horses have large pupils and special cells in their eyes that help them adjust to dim light conditions. This feature allows horses to graze or move around safely, even in low-light conditions. Moreover, horses can see in color, although their color vision is not as developed as humans. Horses can distinguish between shades of yellow, blue, and green, but they cannot see the full range of colors that humans can.

Hearing

As you might guess, horses also have developed a highly sensitive sense of hearing. They have evolved to be able to detect sounds from far distances to help them avoid predators. The ears of horses are flexible and can rotate up to 180 degrees, allowing them to pinpoint the source of a sound. Their hearing is also very acute; horses are able to detect sounds at frequencies up to 33 kHz, compared to humans, who can only hear up to 20 kHz.

Horses also can move each ear independently, allowing them to scan their surroundings for potential danger. When horses feel threatened or unsure, they often point their ears toward the sound to try to identify the potential danger. A very frightened horse may flatten its ears against its head to protect them and reduce the sound they are receiving.

In addition to their acute hearing, horses also can pick up on vibrations through their feet. This allows them to detect the approach of potential predators, even when they cannot hear them. Horses can detect vibrations as low as 16 Hz, which is much lower than what humans are capable of.

Aural Impairment

Horses have evolved a highly sensitive auditory system that allows them to quickly detect any potential threats in their environment. This is why their ears are so large and mobile, with the ability to rotate almost 180 degrees.

However, horses can also suffer from aural impairment, affecting their ability to detect danger and communicate with other horses. Common causes of aural impairment include age, genetics, injury, and infections.

As a horse owner or caretaker, it's important to be aware of any signs of aural impairment in your horse, such as difficulty hearing or responding to sounds, tilting their head to one side, or constantly shaking their head. Regular checkups with your veterinarian can help catch any issues early on and ensure your horse's hearing functions properly.

The Impact of Sound

Loud and sudden noises can be particularly alarming to horses, causing them to become anxious or fearful. This is because their physiology is designed to respond to loud noises as potential threats, even if the sound is not dangerous. This is why it is important for horse owners and handlers to be aware of the impact of sound on horses and be prepared for a horse's reaction to loud or sudden noises in their environment.

Olfaction

Horses have also evolved to rely on their sense of smell as a survival mechanism. They use their sense of smell to detect familiar and calming odors and recognize aversive odors. Here's how it works:

Familiar and Calming Odors

Horses are very sensitive to scents that are familiar to them. They can detect the smell of their herd members from a distance and use it to identify their group. This is why horses often nuzzle each other when they meet—it helps them confirm their identity and feel safe in their surroundings. Similarly, horses can detect familiar scents from their environment, such as hay or grass. These smells are associated with safety and comfort, which can have a calming effect on the horse.

Aversive Odors

On the other hand, horses are also very sensitive to aversive odors, which can signal danger and trigger a flight response. For example, the smell of a predator, blood, or a strong chemical odor can be alarming to a horse. They use their sense of smell to assess their environment and avoid potential threats.

Taste

While the sense of taste in horses is not as well-developed as their other senses, it still plays a role in their survival as prey animals. Horses have taste buds on their tongue, detecting basic flavors such as sweet, salty, sour, and bitter. They are more sensitive to sweet tastes, which may have evolved to help them identify sources of carbohydrates, such as grass and other plants.

Horses have also evolved a behavior called "neophobia," a fear of new foods. This behavior may have developed as a survival mechanism to prevent horses from ingesting toxic plants. By being wary of new foods, horses can avoid consuming something harmful.

Tactile Perception

Tactile perception is a crucial sense for horses as prey animals. They have evolved to be highly sensitive to touch to quickly detect potential threats or predators. Positive tactile stimulation, such as grooming or being scratched, can be rewarding for horses and even strengthen social bonds between herd members. Horses also use touch to communicate with each other, such as nuzzling or nudging.

On the other hand, unpleasant tactile stimulation can cause horses to react quickly and defensively. This can be seen in their reaction to fly bites, where they may stomp their hooves or swish their tails in an attempt to ward off the annoyance. Horses also have sensitive areas on their bodies, such as their flanks and underbelly, that they may be hesitant to let humans touch or groom. Awareness of a horse's tactile sensitivity and preferences is important for creating a positive and respectful relationship with the animal.

In summary, essentially all of a horse's sensory systems have evolved to maximize its ability to survive as a prey animal. Their vision, hearing, and senses of smell and touch are fine-tuned and make them highly sensitive animals.

Other Factors Influencing Perception

Individuality/temperament: Like humans, horses have unique temperaments and personalities. These traits can impact their perception and response to stimuli. Some horses may be more reactive or sensitive, while others may be more relaxed or unresponsive. Understanding your horse's individuality can help you tailor your training and management practices to their needs. Exposure to "scary things" over and over again decreases the severity of a jumpy horse's reactions and should eventually eliminate his fear altogether, but this exposure must be done in a way that does not traumatize the horse or his fear of the object will be worse, not better!

Season and circadian rhythm: Horses are influenced by seasonal changes and their circadian rhythm, or natural sleep-wake cycle. In the summer, they may be more active during the cooler hours of the day and rest during the hotter parts. In the winter, they may require more food and shelter to maintain their body heat. Additionally, horses are crepuscular animals, meaning they are most active during dawn and dusk. Understanding these natural rhythms can help you plan your horse's exercise and care routines for optimal health and well-being.

HISTORY OF HORSES

Horses have a long and fascinating history that dates back to ancient times when they lived in the wild on the grasslands. They were an essential part of the ecosystem, and their survival depended on their ability to adapt to their environment. Horses evolved to be highly sensitive prey animals, with keen senses that allowed them to detect danger from miles away.

However, with the advent of human civilization, the relationship between humans and horses changed. People began to domesticate horses and use them for various purposes, such as transportation, agriculture, and warfare. Today, almost all horses are domesticated and live in a wide range of environments, from farms to urban areas.

The relationship between horses and humans is unique and has been a subject of fascination for centuries. It is a remarkable example of cooperation between two different species that have found a way to communicate and work together toward a common goal.

Horse and Human Relationships

Horses have played a significant role in human history. The domestication of horses began around 4000 BC and revolutionized human society by providing a faster mode of transportation than walking. As a result, horses were used to pull wheeled vehicles, chariots, carts, and wagons, making transporting goods and people much easier.

As time progressed, horses were also trained for riding, which led to their use in battles and hunting. They were instrumental in ancient battles; for example, horses were used by Genghis Khan and his Mongol armies to conquer much of Asia and Europe. The use of horses in warfare in more recent history is well documented, particularly during the settlement of "the West" in the United States both by Native Americans and early European settlers as well as essentially all wars up through World War I in Europe. Additionally, horses have been used extensively all over the world in agriculture to plow fields, transport crops, herd cattle, and perform other ranch work.

While the use of horses for practical tasks like transportation, agriculture, and warfare has diminished over time as technology has evolved, today horses are still used in a variety of ways.

Companionship

One of the most common reasons people keep horses is for companionship. Horses are social animals that thrive in the company of others. They form strong bonds with other horses and the people they interact with.

Work Partnerships

For centuries, horses have been used for transportation, agriculture, and raising livestock like cattle as well as other types of work. They are strong, dependable, and can work long hours without tiring. They can go many places, with a human passenger, that other modes of transportation cannot. The bond between a horse and its owner or handler

is essential in these situations, as they must trust each other to get the job done. While their role in these partnerships is less than it was in times past, many working ranches across the world still prefer to use horses in cattle operations, for example, because of their superiority over mechanized alternatives for many aspects of ranch life. This is also true for in hunting large game in areas with rough terrain.

Competitive Sports

Horses are also used for competitive sports like racing, jumping, dressage, and a multitude of western competitive activities such as roping, reining, cutting, horsemanship and western pleasure competitions, and of course, rodeos. These events require a high level of training, skill, and trust between the horse and rider.

Therapy

Finally, horses are increasingly being used in therapy for individuals with physical, emotional, or mental health issues. This type of therapy, which is often called equine-assisted therapy, has been shown to have many benefits, including improved self-esteem, reduced anxiety, and increased social skills.

Building the Relationship

Building a relationship with a horse can be a truly unique and rewarding experience. Studies have shown that horses can form close bonds with humans and even exhibit positive emotions toward them. To build a strong relationship with your horse, it's important to understand their body language and communication cues. Spend time grooming and caring for your horse, and practice basic ground handling exercises such as leading, lunging, and desensitization. There are hundreds of resources online today where you can find ground work activities – which are activities that you do with a horse while standing on the ground as opposed to riding on the horses back – to help train a horse. This will help establish trust and respect between you and your horse. As you progress to under-saddle work, focus on developing a clear and consistent communication system with your horse through aids and cues. Riding with a relaxed and confident attitude can also help your horse feel more at ease and comfortable in your presence. A successful horse-human relationship is built on trust, respect, and effective communication.

You have reached the end of this chapter on the fascinating history and relationship between horses and humans. You have learned how horses were once wild animals roaming the grasslands and how they have been domesticated and used for various purposes, including transportation, work, sports, and therapy.

You have also discovered how the horse and human relationship forms and functions, with a unique bond beyond mere companionship or utility. Horses have been found to have a special ability to communicate with humans and even help them cope with stress and mental health issues.

IN THE NEXT CHAPTER, we will delve into the life cycle of horses and the different types of horses, including breeds, colors, and sizes. You will learn about the stages of a horse's life, from birth to adulthood, and how they are trained and cared for. Get ready to explore the wonderful world of horses and deepen your understanding of these magnificent creatures!

BORN TO RUN

> *The essential joy of being with horses is that it brings us in contact with the rare elements of grace, beauty, spirit, and fire.*
>
> — SHARON RALLS LEMON

Rooster, Bugzy

Next we will discuss the ins and outs of your horse's life cycle. This is a fun and informative guide to help you better understand your equine companion from birth to old age. By the end of this chapter, you'll have a deeper appreciation for your horse's journey and how to provide the best care for them at every stage. So, saddle up and get ready for a wild ride through the life cycle of horses!

LIFE CYCLE OF A HORSE

In this section, we will delve into the fascinating world of horses and explore their journey from birth to adulthood. We'll cover the five stages of a horse's life, from conception to old age.

The first stage is birth, where a foal is born. Foals are typically born in the spring or early summer and are very cute and fragile. Foals weigh around 100 pounds. They rely on their mother's milk for the first six months of their lives, and they should not be weaned before then.

The second stage is the foal stage, which lasts from birth to about six months old. During this stage, the foal will learn to stand and walk (they generally do this within an hour after birth) and begin to nibble on hay and grains. Foals should be handled gently and given lots of socialization during this stage, as it will help them grow into well-adjusted adults.

The third stage is the weanling stage, which lasts from 6 to 12 months old. This is the stage where the foal is weaned from its mother's milk and learns to eat hay and grains as its primary source of nutrition. The weanling stage is a critical time for growth and development, and it's important to provide your horse with proper nutrition and care.

Rooster as a Yearling

The fourth stage is the yearling stage, which lasts from 1 to 2 years old. During this stage, the horse will continue to grow and develop, and it will begin to exhibit its adult temperament and personality. Yearlings should be trained and handled gently, as they are still learning and growing. Horses should not be ridden until they are at least two years old, at a minimum. Racehorses are often started for riding at 2 years old.

The next stage is adolescence, which lasts from age 2 to 5 years old. This is when most horses are started for riding, but it is important to remember that horses are still growing and developing during this stage. Many ranch horses are started at 3 years old, but your horse may not be ready to carry the load of a rider until he or she is closer to 5 years old. Consult a veterinarian about your horse before you start the horse under saddle.

The final stage is adulthood, which begins at five years old and continues throughout the rest of the horse's life. During adulthood, the horse will continue to grow and mature, and it will be able to be ridden and trained for various activities such as sports, trail riding, and therapy. Providing your horse with proper nutrition and exercise during adulthood is important to keep them healthy and happy.

How Long Do Horses Live?

Horses are beloved animals and companions, and understanding their life expectancy is essential for proper care and planning. The average lifespan of a domesticated horse is between 25 to 30 years. However, this is just an average, and many horses can live well beyond 30 years.

Factors that can influence a horse's life span include genetics, nutrition, exercise, veterinary care, and the living conditions they are subjected to throughout their lives. Horses that receive proper veterinary care and nutrition, live in comfortable and safe environments and receive regular exercise are more likely to live longer and healthier lives.

It's worth noting that horses, like any other animal, can suffer from age-related health issues such as arthritis, dental problems, and digestive issues. Therefore, providing senior horses with appropriate care and support is crucial, including regular veterinary check-ups and a specialized diet that meets their unique nutritional needs is crucial.

How to Tell Your Horse's Age

If you don't have papers or other records to determine a horse's age, one way to estimate it is by examining its teeth. A horse's teeth can give a general idea of its age within a few years. Equine dentists or veterinarians are the best at it, but with practice a novice can also learn to estimate a horse's age based on its teeth.

The easiest way to determine a horse's age is by looking at its incisors, which are the front teeth. The incisors erupt at different times, which can help determine age. Here's what to look for:

- **0-2 years old:** The horse will have baby teeth, also known as deciduous teeth. At birth, the foal will have four incisors on the top and four on the bottom. By the time the horse is two years old, it should have a full set of incisors.
- **3-5 years old:** The horse's teeth will change shape and become oval as they wear down. By the time the horse is five years old, their permanent teeth will erupt, and their mouth will fully develop.
- **6-10 years old:** The horse's teeth will begin to show wear and may begin to develop grooves or cups. These grooves and cups deepen with age, making estimating the horse's age easier.
- **11-15 years old:** The cups on the horse's teeth will begin to disappear, and the teeth will show more wear.

- **16-20 years old:** The teeth will begin to look triangular as they wear down. The horse may begin to lose teeth or have some teeth extracted.
- **21+ years old:** The horse's teeth will be worn down, and they may have lost several teeth. The teeth may also begin to shift and become loose.

It's important to note that this method is not foolproof, and the horse's teeth can be affected by various factors, such as diet and genetics. In addition, horses that are well cared for have their teeth floated, a dental procedure that evens out the horse's teeth and makes it more difficult to estimate their age. The purpose of floating is to remove sharp points that have developed on the teeth, and encourage an even grinding pattern to aid in digestion.

If you're unsure of a horse's age, it's always best to consult a veterinarian or equine dentist who can give you a more accurate estimate.

TYPES OF HORSES

Let's look into some of the most common types of horses. There is a huge variety of different kinds of horses which are all used for many different purposes. The physical and mental traits of the different horse types are what allow them to all succeed in certain equestrian disciplines.

Light Horses

Light horses are commonly used for riding, racing, showing, and driving. They are agile, fast, and versatile animals and come in a wide range of breeds. Some popular light horse breeds include Thoroughbreds, Quarter Horses, Arabians, and Standardbreds.

Ranch

Ranch horses, also known as working horses, are bred and trained for various tasks related to ranching and farming. These horses are sturdy, reliable, and have excellent stamina, which makes them perfect for long hours of work on the ranch. They are typically used for herding cattle, pulling plows and wagons, and other ranch-related activities. Ranch horses are often intelligent and have a strong work ethic, making them an excellent choice for experienced riders who require a horse that can handle a range of tasks.

Riding

Riding horses are bred and trained specifically for recreational riding, such as trail riding, jumping, dressage, and pleasure riding. These horses are typically well-mannered and easy to handle, making them ideal for novice riders.

Racing

Racing horses are bred and trained for speed, endurance, and agility, with Thoroughbreds being the most common breed used for racing. These horses are highly competitive and often raced on flat tracks, over jumps, and turf. Interesting fact: the American Quarter Horse is actually faster than a Thoroughbred over the quarter mile distance, which is how it got its name.

Showing

Showing horses are bred and trained to compete in horse shows, such as dressage, jumping, and halter classes. These horses are evaluated based on their conformation, movement, and performance. Conformation is discussed later in this chapter, but the term essentially refers to the assessment of how a horse's physical features, movement, and behavior affect its suitability for a particular task, or job. The concept is similar to how dogs are judged at dog shows.

Driving

Driving horses are bred and trained for carriage or cart driving. These horses are typically larger and stronger than riding horses and are trained to pull carriages, carts, and other vehicles either for work. This can be jobs like carriage rides for tourists (think Central Park in New York City, or Western carriage rides in the American West), cart jobs in agriculture, or for competitions like racing or general pulling competitions.

Miniature

Miniature horses are smaller than regular horses and are often kept as pets, or used in therapy programs. Despite their small size, they are strong and intelligent animals and can be trained to pull carts or perform other tasks.

Draft Horses

Draft horses are the largest type of horse, weighing over 1,500 pounds. They are bred for their strength and are primarily used for heavy work, such as plowing fields, pulling heavy loads, and logging. These horses are also sometimes used to pull carts (as described in the Driving section above), but generally not cart racing. They have a gentle temperament and are known for their calmness, making them ideal for beginner riders.

Ponies

Ponies are smaller horses that are less than 14.2 hands (58 inches) in height. They are known for their endurance, hardiness, strength and sure-footedness. They are versatile and used for various activities such as riding, driving, jumping, and work and are often popular with children. And, in my experience though, they can often have quite an attitude!

Coldblood

Coldblood horses are large, heavy horses that originated in northern Europe. They are bred for their strength and are used for heavy work, such as plowing and hauling. They are known for their calm temperament and are often used as riding horses.

Hotblood

Hotblood horses, with a sleek, elegant appearance, are generally smaller and more refined than other breeds. They have a high level of energy and are highly sensitive to their surroundings, making them highly responsive to their rider's commands.

The most famous hotblood breeds include the Arabian, the Thoroughbred, and the Akhal-Teke.

Cob

Cob horses are small, sturdy horses often used for driving and riding. They have a muscular build, a broad chest, and strong legs. They are known for their calm temperament and are often used as beginner horses.

Hack

Hack horses are a type of riding horse that is bred for their ability to move with style and grace. They are typically used in English riding disciplines, such as jumping and dressage. They have a refined appearance and are known for their athleticism and agility.

WHAT ARE ALL THESE DIFFERENT NAMES FOR YOUNG HORSES?

In the equine world, young horses have various names, depending on their age and gender. Here are the different terms you need to know:

Foal

A foal is a baby horse that is less than one year old. Foals can stand up and walk within an hour of birth and start nursing from their mothers immediately.

Weanlings

Weanlings are foals between six and twelve months old and have been weaned from their mother's milk. They are learning to eat grass and hay and may also start to be trained to wear a halter and lead rope.

Yearlings

Yearlings are horses that are one year old. They are still considered babies and are not fully grown. They may be trained to wear a saddle and bridle but are not typically ridden until they are at least two years old.

Colt

A colt is a male horse that is less than four years old. Colts are generally gelded (castrated) if they are not intended for breeding.

Filly

A filly is a female horse that is less than four years old.

Knowing the different terms for young horses can help you better understand and appreciate the different stages of a horse's life – and be able to "speak horse" with others.

HOW ARE HORSES DIFFERENT FROM ...?

Feral horses, donkeys, and mules are all closely related to horses but have some distinct differences.

Feral horses:

- Feral horses live in the wild and are descendants of domesticated horses that have escaped or been released.
- They are typically smaller than domesticated horses and have leaner, more compact bodies.
- They have stronger hooves and can run faster and longer than most domesticated horses.

- They can survive in harsh environments, making them well-adapted to life in the wild.

Donkeys:

- Donkeys are closely related to horses and are members of the equine family but have several physical and behavioral differences.
- They are smaller than horses and have long ears, short mane, and bristly coats.
- They are known for being strong and sure-footed and are often used as pack animals.
- They have a reputation for being stubborn but are highly intelligent and have a strong sense of self-preservation.

Mules:

- Mules are a cross between a male donkey and a female horse.
- They have a combination of characteristics from both parents, such as the long ears and sure-footedness of a donkey and the strength and size of a horse.
- They are often used as working animals, such as for plowing fields or hauling heavy loads.
- They are known for being intelligent and adaptable, but they can also be stubborn and require a skilled handler.
- They are sterile and, therefore, unable to produce any offspring of their own.

TOP BREEDS OF HORSES

As mentioned earlier, there are more than 350 breeds, so this list is far from extensive but it will give you an introduction to some of the most well-known breeds.

American Quarter Horse

The American Quarter Horse is one of the most popular breeds in America. They are known for their muscular build, speed, and agility. They are versatile and used for various activities such as racing, rodeo events, and ranch work. They are usually between 14 and 16 hands tall and weigh between 950 and 1,200 pounds. They are also one of my favorite two favorite breeds, which is why they get to be listed first in this section.

American Paint Horse

The American Paint Horse is another popular breed in America. This breed combines the conformational characteristics of a western stock horse with a pinto spotting pattern of white are dark coat colors. These horses are developed from Quarter Horse and Thoroughbred bloodlines. And, they are the second of my two favorite breeds. But, I'm from Montana, so I am probably biased.

Arabian

The Arabian horse is one of the oldest breeds, originating from the Arabian Peninsula. They have a distinctive head shape and are known for their endurance, intelligence, and gentle temperament. They are used for various activities such as racing, endurance riding, and horse shows. They are usually between 14 and 16 hands tall and weigh between 800 and 1,000 pounds.

Thoroughbred

The Thoroughbred is a popular breed in the racing world. They are known for their speed, agility, and athleticism. They are usually between 15 and 17 hands tall and weigh between 1,000 and 1,200 pounds. They are used for various activities such as racing, show jumping, and dressage.

Appaloosa

The Appaloosa horse is known for its distinctive spotted coat pattern. They are usually between 14 and 16 hands tall and weigh between 950 and 1,250 pounds. They are versatile and used for various activities such as trail riding, ranch work, and horse shows. Several horsemen that live in and operate different horse-related tourism businesses in Western Montana have told me that Appaloosa horses exhibit the most "toughness" of any breed that they have worked with, meaning they can work long hard days better than any other trail horses. That of course is anecdotal, but still very interesting to hear from multiple people.

Morgan

The Morgan horse is a versatile breed known for its strength, stamina, and calm temperament. They are used for various activities such as driving, dressage, and trail riding. They are usually between 14 and 16 hands tall and weigh between 900 and 1,200 pounds.

Warmbloods

Warmbloods are a group of breeds that have a combination of hot and cold-blooded traits. They are bred for their athletic ability and used for show jumping, dressage, and eventing. They are usually between 15 and 17 hands tall and weigh between 1,100 and 1,400 pounds.

Gaited Breeds

Gaited breeds are breeds that have a natural, smooth gait. They are used for various activities such as trail riding, endurance riding, and horse shows. Some examples include the Tennessee Walking Horse and the Paso Fino.

Draft Breeds

Draft breeds are known for their strength and size. They are used for various activities, such as pulling heavy loads and driving and generally weigh between 1,400 and 2,000 pounds. Some examples include the Clydesdale (think beer commercials!), the Percheron, and the Belgian Draft.

Grade Horses

Grade horses are horses of mixed breeding that do not belong to any specific breed, and therefore cannot be registered. They are versatile and used for various activities like trail riding and ranch work.

IN THIS CHAPTER, you learned about the different aspects of horses, from their life cycle and age to their various types and breeds. You discovered that horses have a complex and fascinating life cycle, with distinct stages that bring changes in their behavior, appearance, and abilities. You also explored the diverse types of horses, ranging from miniature to draft horses, each with specific characteristics and uses.

Now that you have a good understanding of the different aspects of horses, the next chapter will take a closer look at their anatomy. You will learn about the various body parts of a horse, from their head to their hooves, and how these parts function together to enable horses to perform various tasks, from running and jumping to carrying a rider. You'll also start to learn how to care for different part of your horse and ensure that he stays healthy and happy. So, get ready to dive deeper into the fascinating world of horses' anatomy!

THE BLUEPRINT OF A HORSE

A horse is the projection of peoples' dreams about themselves--strong, powerful, beautiful--and it has the capability of giving us escape from our mundane existence.

— PAM BROWN

Tater, American Paint Horse

A s a horse owner or enthusiast, it's important to understand their physical makeup to ensure their health and well-being. This chapter will delve into the various parts of a horse's anatomy and how they impact its movement, temperament, and overall behavior. Understanding the anatomy of a horse will not only make you a better caretaker, but it will also deepen your appreciation for these wonderful animals.

ANATOMY OF A HORSE

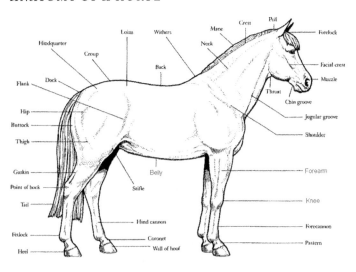

Understanding the anatomy of a horse is essential for anyone involved in caring for and managing these majestic animals. Whether you are a horse owner, trainer, rider, or just someone interested in horses, this section will provide you with a comprehensive overview of the anatomy of a horse and how it affects its behavior.

Horses' Heads

The head of a horse is one of its most distinguishing features. It is also the part of the horse that communicates the most to humans. The head includes the poll, which is the area behind the ears, and the forehead, which is above the eyes.

Horses' Eyes

Horses' eyes are located on the side of their head, and they have a wide field of vision. The horse's vision is monocular, meaning they can see with each eye independently. Horses use their eyes to detect movement and have excellent night vision.

Horses' Teeth

Horses have four types of teeth, including incisors, canines, premolars, and molars. It is essential to care for a horse's teeth by providing them with proper dental care to avoid dental problems.

Horses' Necks

A horse's neck is an essential part of its body that plays a crucial role in the animal's movement, balance, and overall health. A horse's neck consists of seven cervical vertebrae, which are connected by ligaments, muscles, and tendons. A horse's neck is also home to the animal's windpipe, esophagus, major blood vessels, and spinal cord.

Horses' Barrel and Withers

A horse's barrel refers to its body from the end of the ribcage to the beginning of the hindquarters. The spine and ribcage support it and contain vital organs such as the heart, lungs, and digestive system. The shape and size of the barrel can vary greatly among breeds, and it is an important consideration for riders when selecting a saddle that fits the horse properly.

The withers are the bony protrusions located at the base of the horse's neck, just above the shoulder blades. They serve as the attachment point for the horse's neck, back, and shoulder muscles and are an important landmark for determining saddle fit. The height and slope of the withers can also vary among breeds. Additionally, the withers are the point where a horse's height is measured. In the equine world, height is measured in "hands," with one hand equaling four inches. So, for example, a horse that stands 15 hands high is 60 inches, or five feet, at the withers. Understanding the importance of the withers can help you ensure proper saddle fit and accurately measure your horse's height.

When selecting a saddle, it is important to ensure that it fits the horse's barrel and withers properly to avoid causing discomfort or injury. The shape and angle of the saddle tree should match the horse's back, and the gullet should be wide enough to provide clearance for the withers. A poorly fitting saddle can cause soreness, stiffness, open sores and scars from rubbing, and even lameness in the horse.

Horses' Chest

The chest of a horse is the front part of its body between the forelegs, and it plays a vital role in the horse's overall physical development and movement. A well-developed chest can help the horse to breathe more efficiently, and it also contributes to the horse's overall balance and strength.

Anatomy of Horses' Chests

The chest is comprised of several components, including the sternum, ribs, and muscles. The sternum is a long, flat bone in the middle of the chest, which provides the attachment for the horse's ribs. The ribs are attached to the sternum at one end and the spine at the other. The chest muscles, such as the pectorals, intercostals, and serratus ventralis, provide the horse with the strength and stability needed for various activities.

Horses' Flank

The flank is the area of the horse's body between the ribs and the hip. It is a large and muscular area that can be easily seen when the horse moves. The flank is an important part of the horse's anatomy as it houses many vital organs, such as the kidneys and reproductive organs.

Horses' Spine/Back

The spine or back of a horse is a crucial part of its anatomy. It runs from the poll to the end of the tail. The section of the spine between the withers and the croup is composed of 54 to 58 vertebrae, although some breeds, such as draft horses, may have more. The horse's spine is divided into three regions: the cervical spine, which includes the neck vertebrae; the thoracic spine, which includes the withers and rib cage; and the lumbar spine, which includes the lower back and loin. Each region has its own unique characteristics that affect the horse's movement, balance, and overall health.

Understanding the anatomy of the horse's spine can help you better care for your horse and identify potential issues early on.

- **Straight Back:** A straight back is a relatively flat spine with few curves. This type of back is ideal for riding and can comfortably support a rider's weight.
- **Sway Back:** A swayback, also known as lordosis, is a spine with an excessive curve. Various factors, including genetics, age, and poor conformation can cause this. Horses with sway backs may experience difficulty carrying weight, and their spine may be more susceptible to injury.
- **Roach Back:** A roach back, also known as kyphosis, is a spine with a pronounced upward curve. Horses with roach backs may have difficulty carrying weight and may experience discomfort when ridden.

It is essential to remember that the spine is a sensitive area and can be easily injured. Always ensure your horse is properly fitted with a saddle and that your riding technique does not cause unnecessary stress to your horse's back. Regular veterinary check-ups and proper training can also help prevent back injuries in horses.

Anatomy of Front and Back Limbs in Horses

Understanding the anatomy of a horse's limbs is crucial for any horse owner or rider. Horses are highly athletic animals; their limbs support their weight while enabling them to run, jump, and navigate various terrains.

Function and Build of Front Limbs

The front limbs of horses are composed of various bones, muscles, tendons, and ligaments. The horse's shoulder blade, humerus bone, radius, ulna, and carpal bones comprise its front limb. The shoulder blade is essential for shock absorption, and the humerus connects the shoulder blade and the elbow joint. The radius and ulna form the forearm, and the carpal bones make up the horse's wrist.

The front limb's primary function is to support the horse's weight and absorb shock when the horse moves or jumps. The horse's front limbs are also responsible for initiating movement and maintaining balance when the horse is in motion. The horse's front limbs have a different structure and function than their back limbs, as their front limbs have more significant bones and joints that support the weight and absorb impact.

Function and Build of Back Limbs

The back limbs of horses consist of the femur bone, tibia bone, fibula, and tarsal bones. The femur bone is the largest in the horse's body, connecting the hip and the stifle joint. The stifle joint is similar to the human knee joint, and the tibia and fibula make up the horse's lower leg. The tarsal bones form the hock joint, which is comparable to the human ankle joint.

The back limb's primary function is to propel the horse forward and provide support when the horse is in motion. The back limbs' powerful muscles, tendons, and ligaments allow the horse to generate and transfer energy from the hindquarters to the front limbs. The horse's back limbs are also responsible for maintaining balance and direction when the horse is in motion.

Types of Postures

Horses have different postures depending on their breed, age, and activity level. A horse's posture can provide insight into the horse's mood, comfort level, and health. The three primary horse postures are the square stance, camped-out stance, and parked-out stance.

The square stance is the most relaxed posture, where the horse stands with all four feet square on the ground. In the camped-out stance, the horse places its back feet further back than its front feet, indicating readiness to move. The parked-out stance is where the horse stands with its front feet further forward than its back feet, indicating relaxation or discomfort.

Faults, Anomalies, and Ailments in Horse Pastern

Conformation Faults of Forelegs

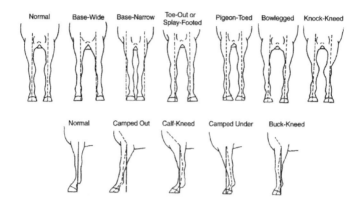

The pastern is the area between the hoof and the fetlock joint in a horse's limb. Faults, anomalies, and ailments in the horse's pastern can cause lameness, discomfort, and pain. Some common faults include long, sloping pasterns, short upright pasterns, and too much or too little angle between the pastern and the hoof. Anomalies, such as contracted or collapsed pasterns, can be congenital or acquired.

Ailments in the pastern can include arthritis, tendon and ligament damage, and fractures. Proper hoof care, regular exercise, and appropriate nutrition can help prevent many of these issues.

Croup

The croup is the area on the horse's hindquarters between the loin and the base of the tail. It is an important part of the horse's anatomy as it is the foundation for the hindquarters and determines the horse's ability to extend its hind legs and push off the ground. The slope and length of the croup also affect the horse's balance and overall movement.

Types of croups: Different types of croups can affect the horse's performance and suitability for different disciplines. A level croup is ideal for dressage and jumping, while a sloping croup is better for western disciplines like reining and cutting.

Tail

The horse's tail is a continuation of the spine and provides balance, communication, and fly protection. It is also important to the horse's appearance and breed characteristics.

Types of tails: Different breeds of horses have different types of tails. For example, Arabians have a high-set tail, while Quarter Horses have a low-set tail. The thickness and length of the tail can also vary, with some horses having a thicker and longer tail for better fly protection.

Maintaining the tail: Maintaining the horse's tail by regularly cleaning it and detangling any knots or mats is important. Some horse owners also choose to trim their horse's tails for better hygiene and appearance.

HOW DO HORSES RUN SO FAST?

Here are some key points to help you understand the role of certain organs and muscles in making horses run faster:

- **Slow-twitch muscles:** Horses have a high proportion of slow-twitch muscles in their bodies, which allow them to maintain their speed over long distances without fatigue.
- **Spleen:** Horses have an unusually large spleen, which can store and release large amounts of oxygen-rich red blood cells during exercise. This helps the horse to maintain its speed for longer periods.
- **Big hearts:** Horses have relatively large hearts compared to other animals, which enables them to pump more blood with each beat. This means that the horse's muscles receive more oxygen, which increases their endurance and allows them to run faster for longer periods. For example, the famous racehorse Secretariat had a heart weighing approximately 22 pounds, about three times the size of an average horse's heart. This contributed to his exceptional speed and stamina, along with other anatomical factors such as his large lungs and strong hindquarters.
- **Latherin:** Horses produce a substance called latherin which creates a frothy sweat that helps to cool the horse's body during exercise. This allows the horse to maintain its speed for longer periods without overheating.
- **Respiratory tract:** Horses have a highly efficient respiratory system that allows them to take in large amounts of oxygen and expel carbon dioxide quickly.

This means that the horse's muscles receive more oxygen, which increases their endurance and allows them to run faster for longer periods.

- **Bones:** Horses have relatively lightweight but strong bones in their legs, which help to absorb the shock of running at high speeds without breaking.
- **Tough hooves:** Horses have tough, resilient hooves that can withstand the impact of running at high speeds over varied terrain. This enables the horse to run faster and more confidently without risking injury.
- **Breath power:** A horse's breathing power is critical for its speed and endurance. The horse's lungs need to be able to take in and process large amounts of oxygen to supply the muscles during exercise. The horse's diaphragm and intercostal muscles help to draw air in and out of the lungs quickly and efficiently.

By understanding the importance of these various organs and muscles, we can appreciate the remarkable capabilities of horses and why they are able to run so fast.

HORSE HOOF ANATOMY

If you know anyone who has knowledge about horses, the one thing 98% of them will say is "no hoof, no horse". This saying in meant to convey the fact that the number one most important part of a horse's anatomy are its hooves. Hoof health, conformation, and consistent care are essential to a horse's well-being.

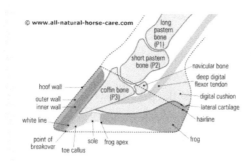

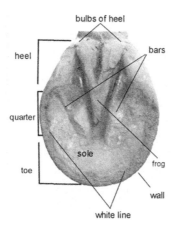

Horse hooves are an essential part of a horse's anatomy, providing support, traction, and shock absorption during movement. Understanding the structure and function of hooves is crucial for maintaining horse health and preventing lameness. In this section, we will discuss the types, build, and purpose of horse hooves.

Types and Build of Hooves

Horse hooves come in various shapes and sizes, depending on the breed, activity level, and environment. The two main types of hooves are:

- **Barefoot hooves**: Barefoot hooves refer to hooves that do not have horseshoes attached to them. Horses with strong, healthy hooves can perform well without shoes.
- **Shod hooves**: Horses that work on hard surfaces or have hoof problems require shoes for protection and support. Horseshoes are made of various materials, such as steel, aluminum, and plastic, and come in different shapes and sizes to fit the horse's hoof. Many people also shoe horses with specialized shoes in the winter in Northern climates if the horses are ridden in icy conditions.

Purpose of Hooves

The hooves play a vital role in a horse's overall health and well-being. Here are some essential functions of horse hooves:

- **Support**: The hooves' primary function is to provide support for the horse's body weight and absorb shock when the horse moves.
- **Shock absorption**: Hooves absorb shock during movement, protecting the horse's bones and joints from injury.
- **Traction**: Hooves provide traction, allowing the horse to grip the ground and move smoothly.

- **Blood circulation**: The frog, located in the center of the hoof, pumps blood with each step, promoting healthy blood circulation.
- **Sensory perception**: The hoof has nerve endings that provide sensory feedback to the horse's brain, allowing it to adjust its movements and maintain balance.
- **Defense:** Lastly, hooves also serve as a defense mechanism against predators.

Importance of a Healthy Hoof for a Horse

A horse's hooves play a vital role in its overall health and well-being. Here are some important aspects to consider:

Anatomy of Horse Hooves

- **Composition**: Hooves are made up of keratinized tissue, which is a protein similar to human hair and nails. It consists of three main parts:
- **The outer layer**: The outer layer is the hoof wall, made of keratin, a tough protein. It covers the entire hoof and protects the sensitive structures inside.
- **The middle layer**: The middle layer is the hoof's internal structure, consisting of laminae, which connect the hoof wall to the coffin bone. The laminae provide support and shock absorption during movement.
- **The inner layer**: The inner layer is the soft tissue inside the hoof, including the frog, sole, and digital cushion. The frog is a V-shaped structure that absorbs shock and prevents slipping. The sole

protects the internal structures and helps with weight distribution. The digital cushion is a shock-absorbing pad between the hoof wall and the coffin bone.

Functional Anatomy of Horse Foot

- **Basic Anatomy**: The horse's foot is composed of the coffin bone, navicular bone, and a complex system of ligaments, tendons, and blood vessels. These structures work together to support the horse's weight, absorb shock, and facilitate movement.
- **Frog**: The frog is the V-shaped structure on the bottom of the hoof. It acts as a shock absorber and helps pump blood back up the horse's leg.
- **Sole**: The sole is the flat surface of the hoof that protects the sensitive inner structures.
- **White Line**: The white line is the area where the outer hoof wall meets the sole. It provides support to the coffin bone.

Hooves of a Foal

- **Eponychium**: The eponychium, also known as "fairy fingers," is a soft, fleshy tissue that covers the hooves of foals. It protects the growing hoof from the mare's uterus and prevents infection.

- **Importance of Hoof Care**: Foals' hooves grow rapidly, and proper care is essential to ensure healthy growth and development.

Hoof Care for Foals

- **Regular Trimming**: Regular trimming is especially important for foals, as their hooves grow quickly and require frequent attention to prevent overgrowth and promote proper development. It's also a good idea to get young horses accustomed to regular trimming and handling while they are smaller and more manageable than full-size adult horses. This helps them develop good manners and makes it easier for them to receive proper hoof care throughout their lives. By starting early with regular hoof trimming, you can help ensure your horse's health and well-being for years to come.
- **Proper Nutrition**: Proper nutrition is crucial for healthy hoof growth in foals. A balanced diet with

adequate protein, vitamins, and minerals is necessary.

Why Do Horses Need Shoes?

It's important to note that not all horses need shoes, and some horses do just fine without them. However, horseshoes can provide several benefits for horses who do need them. They can protect the hooves from excessive wear and tear caused by rough terrain and provide additional traction on slippery surfaces like ice or mud. Additionally, shoes can help correct structural or gait issues in horses, making them more comfortable and preventing further damage to their hooves or legs. If you're unsure whether your horse needs shoes, it's a good idea to consult your veterinarian or farrier for guidance.

- **Purpose of Shoes**: Horseshoes protect the hooves from excessive wear and tear, provide additional traction, and help correct structural or gait issues. Many horses that are used in various types of competitions often wear shoes.
- **Proper Fitting**: It's important to ensure that horseshoes are properly fitted to your horse's hooves. Poorly fitted shoes can cause pain, discomfort, and even injury to the horse. To ensure that your horse's shoes are fitted correctly, it's recommended that you hire a professional farrier who is experienced in trimming and shoeing horses. If you are reading this book, I assume you are just starting out in the world of horses. DO NOT attempt to shoe your own

horses. I know that YouTube videos are great these days, but you not only can, but probably WILL seriously hurt your horse if you attempt to do this yourself. Remember – no hoof, no horse! Do not even attempt to trim your own horses, always hire a professional. Regular maintenance and adjustments to shoes if your horse wears them can help ensure your horse's comfort and well-being. If you notice any signs of discomfort or lameness in your horse, it's important to consult with your veterinarian or farrier as soon as possible to address the issue.

Do Horseshoes Hurt Horses?

- **Nailing Process**: Horseshoes are attached to the hooves with nails, and the nailing process can cause discomfort if not done correctly.
- **Proper Fitting**: Properly fitted horseshoes should not cause pain or discomfort to the horse. Regular maintenance and adjustments can ensure the horse's comfort and well-being. One of my horses does occasionally wear shoes – and he actually dozes off during the process. So, no – shoeing a horse, when done correctly, does not cause him pain.

IN THIS CHAPTER, we explored the anatomy of a horse, examining each body part and its role in the horse's overall function. We discussed the importance of understanding a horse's anatomy and how it can affect its performance and health. We covered topics such as the horse's head, neck, chest, back, limbs, and hooves, detailing their structure and function. We also delved into the significance of a healthy hoof, explaining what horse hooves are made of, their functional anatomy, and why horses may need horseshoes.

As you continue reading, keep in mind the importance of understanding a horse's anatomy and how it plays a role in its health and performance. Additionally, consider the benefits and challenges of horse ownership as you evaluate whether owning a horse is the right decision for you.

THE BEAUTY AND THE BURDEN

O wning a horse can bring about many benefits, both physical and emotional. In this chapter, we will explore how horses can increase happiness in their owners. From the therapeutic benefits of riding to the simple joys of spending time with your equine companion, there are countless reasons why owning a horse can bring happiness into your life. However, as with any major decision, there are also drawbacks to consider. In the following pages, we will examine the pros and cons of horse ownership so that you can make an informed decision about whether owning a horse is right for you.

WHY OWNING A HORSE IS SO FULFILLING

Are you considering owning a horse? Well, you're in for a treat! Here are some reasons why owning a horse can be such a fulfilling experience.

- **Keeps you physically active**: Horses require a lot of physical care, including grooming, feeding, and exercising. Caring for a horse can be a great way to get outside and stay active. You'll be getting plenty of fresh air and exercise, which can benefit your physical and mental health.
- **Builds self-confidence**: Owning a horse can be a great way to build self-confidence. As you learn to care for your horse and ride them, you'll gain a sense of pride and accomplishment. Horses are also very intuitive animals, and they can sense your emotions. Building a trusting relationship with your horse can be a great confidence booster.
- **Reduces stress**: Spending time with horses can be incredibly calming and therapeutic. Being around these animals can help you relax and reduce stress. Many people find that spending time with horses is a great way to escape the stresses of everyday life.
- **Keeps you socially active**: Owning a horse can be a great way to meet new people and make friends. You can join local riding clubs or attend events and shows with your horse. This can be a great way to connect with like-minded people who share your love of horses.
- **Helps disabled individuals stay active**: Horses can be incredibly therapeutic for people with disabilities. Riding can be a great way to improve balance, coordination, and muscle strength. It can also be a great way to boost confidence and self-esteem.
- **Engages the creative side of your brain**: Owning a horse can be a very creative experience. You'll need

to devise different ways to keep your horse entertained and stimulated. This can involve designing obstacle courses, creating new riding routes, or making homemade treats for your horse.

- **Builds character**: Owning a horse can be a great way to build character. It requires a lot of responsibility, patience, and dedication. Learning to care for and ride your horse can be a great way to develop important life skills that will serve you well in other areas.

- **You learn better time management**: Owning a horse requires a lot of time and effort. You'll need to learn how to manage your time effectively to ensure your horse is well cared for. This can be a great way to develop better time management skills that will serve you well in other areas of your life.

- **It promotes a union with nature**: Horses are incredibly connected to nature, and spending time with them can help you to feel more connected to the natural world. Riding through fields and forests can be a great way to appreciate the beauty of nature and escape the hustle and bustle of modern life.

- **Maintains bone mass**: Riding horses can be a great way to maintain bone mass and prevent osteoporosis. The impact of the horse's movement can help to strengthen bones and prevent bone loss.

- **Improves digestion**: Spending time outside with horses can also be beneficial for digestion. The fresh air and exercise can help to stimulate digestion and keep your gut healthy.

Overall, owning a horse can be an incredibly fulfilling experience. From staying physically active to building self-confidence, owning a horse can offer a wide range of benefits for both your physical and mental health. Why not consider adding a horse to your family?

THE REALITIES OF OWNING A HORSE

Before you dive headfirst into horse ownership, it's important to understand the realities of caring for these animals. Here are some things to consider:

- **It costs money—all of it**: Owning a horse is expensive. The cost of actual horse is only the beginning. There is feed, farrier services, veterinary care, equipment, and stabling or boarding fees if you don't own our own land. The expenses can quickly add up. It's important to be financially prepared for the costs of horse ownership.
- **Horses can teach responsibility – and that means you're expending time and energy**: Owning a horse can be a great way to learn responsibility because it requires significant time and effort. Caring for a horse requires daily attention. This can be a great way to develop a strong work ethic and sense of responsibility. It's important to be prepared to dedicate a large portion of your time to caring for your horse, including feeding, grooming, and exercise.
- **Injuries**: Unfortunately, horses can be prone to injuries. Whether it's a minor cut or a more serious

injury, it's important to be prepared to handle medical emergencies. This can be both stressful and expensive.

- **Sicknesses**: Horses can be susceptible to sickness, including respiratory illnesses, colic, and laminitis. These illnesses can be both stressful and expensive to treat.
- **Horses are great for exercise**: Riding a horse can be a great form of exercise. It can help to improve balance, coordination, and muscle strength. However, it's important to remember that owning a horse also requires physical labor, including cleaning stalls, lifting hay bales, and carrying water buckets.
- **Finding quality feed/hay in down years**: The cost of feed and hay can vary depending on the time of year and availability. During down years, finding high-quality feed and hay at an affordable price can be difficult.
- **Training them can be frustrating**: Training a horse can be a frustrating experience. Horses are intelligent animals, and they can also be stubborn and difficult to work with. It's important to be patient and consistent when training a horse.
- **The dirty jobs**: Caring for a horse also involves some dirty jobs, including cleaning stalls, mucking out manure, and grooming your horse. While these tasks may not be glamorous, they are an essential part of horse ownership.

Just remember, owning a horse can be a rewarding and fulfilling experience, but it's essential to be prepared for the realities of caring for these animals. From the financial costs to the physical labor and emotional stress, horse ownership requires a significant commitment. But for those who are passionate about horses, the rewards can be well worth it. If you're ready for the challenge, owning a horse can be a wonderful addition to your life.

WHAT IF YOU DON'T HAVE THE RESOURCES TO OWN A HORSE?

Not having the resources to own a horse doesn't mean you can't be involved with these amazing animals. Here are some ways to get involved:

- **You're not alone**: There are many horse lovers out there just like you who cannot afford to own a horse. Don't feel alone, and know there are still ways to get involved.
- **Volunteer**: Volunteering at a rescue or a therapeutic riding center can be a great way to be around horses without the expense of owning one. Not only will you be able to care for and work with horses, but you will also be helping an organization that provides an important service to the community.
- **Get a horse job**: If you have experience working with horses, consider getting a job at a local barn or stable. You may be able to earn some money while also getting the chance to work with horses.
- **Do a horse lease, share, or loan**: Leasing, sharing, or loaning a horse can be a great option if you cannot afford one on your own. These arrangements can

vary, but they all involve sharing the cost of owning a horse with someone else.

- **Take lessons**: Taking riding lessons can be a great way to learn about horses and improve your riding skills. Most riding schools provide their own horses, so you won't have to worry about the expense of owning a horse.

- **Make friends with horse people**: By making friends with horse people, you may be able to get involved with horses more informally. Many horse owners are happy to share their passion with others and may allow you to spend time with their horses.

- **Go watch local shows**: Watching local horse shows can be a fun and informative way to learn about horses and meet other horse enthusiasts. You may even be able to volunteer at the event and help out behind the scenes.

- **Not now doesn't mean not ever**: If owning a horse is a dream of yours, remember that it doesn't have to happen right now. Keep saving money, continue to learn about horses, and stay involved in the horse community. With time and effort, you may be able to own a horse in the future.

- **The 4H horse program**: If you're between the ages of 8 and 18, or if you have kids that are, the 4H horse program can be a great way to learn about horses and get involved with the horse community. This program provides educational opportunities and the chance to compete in horse shows and other events. Many 4H programs have horses that participants can use, so you won't have to worry about owning your own horse.

IN THIS CHAPTER, we've explored the many benefits of owning a horse, from physical fitness to emotional fulfillment. We've also discussed the challenges and realities of horse ownership, from the costs involved to the time and effort required to properly care for these animals. But even if you don't have the resources to own a horse, there are still plenty of ways to get involved with the horse community and experience the joy of being around these amazing animals.

In the next chapter, we'll dive deeper into the process of buying your first horse. We'll discuss the important factors to consider, from breed and age to temperament and training, and we'll offer practical tips for finding and selecting the perfect horse for you. If you're ready to take the next step on your horse journey, stay tuned for our guide on how to buy your first horse!

HORSE SENSE

> *Riding a horse is not a gentle hobby to be picked up*
> *and laid down like a game of Solitaire. It is a grand*
> *passion. It seizes a person whole and once it has done*
> *so, he/she will have to accept that his life will be radi-*
> *cally changed.*

— RALPH WALDO EMERSON

W hether you're a seasoned rider or completely new to the horse world, the process of buying your own horse can be both exhilarating and overwhelming. There are a lot of factors to consider, from breed and age to temperament and training, and it's important to approach the buying process with a clear understanding of what you're looking for and what you can realistically handle.

In this chapter, we'll guide you through the process of buying your first horse, offering practical tips and expert advice to help you find the perfect horse for your needs and goals.

From assessing your riding experience to evaluating potential horses, we'll cover everything you need to know to make an informed and confident purchase.

HOW TO BUY YOUR FIRST HORSE

You've decided to purchase a horse, but where do you even buy one from? Well, to start with, a thorough online search can be a good way to find out what your perfect horse is selling for and if there are any suitable horses for sale near you. But wait, what are your requirements? Let's look at some of the things you should consider before going horse shopping.

Age

When it comes to buying a horse, one of the key decisions you'll need to make is their age. There are advantages and disadvantages to buying a horse at different ages, so it's important to carefully consider your options.

Young horses, which include foals up to three years old, can be a tempting choice if you want to start from scratch and develop a strong bond with your horse from an early age. However, it's important to note that young horses require specialized care and attention, including regular vet checkups, proper nutrition, and careful handling to avoid injury. But, even more importantly, they require training. Be prepared to pay a trainer if you get a young horse. It can be a lot of work, but seeing your young horse grow and develop into a well-trained and loyal partner can also be incredibly rewarding.

Adolescent horses, which are typically between three and five years old, can be a good compromise between a young horse and an older, more experienced one. These horses are still developing physically and mentally, but they may have some basic training and handling already under their belt. When looking at adolescent horses, be sure to consider their training, temperament, as well as any past experiences they may have had. That being said, I would not necessarily recommend a horse this young for a beginner. However, it is an option provided you understand what you are getting yourself in to.

Older horses are generally a great choice for first-time horse buyers who want a more seasoned partner. I personally think this is the best option for a new horse owner. You want a "been there, done that" kind of horse. To put a number on it, I would say look for a horse that is at least ten years old. Even older is fine if the horse is in good physical condition. Look for an older horse who is already well-trained and has a laid-back temperament. This will allow you to gain confidence as you learn to be around horses, and eventually learn to ride. Remember, the more nervous you are the more nervous the horse will be, and older horses who have had exposure to lots of experiences and riders generally have more tolerance for inexperienced riders and are therefore less likely to get jumpy or spooked if you are a little bit nervous. However, it's important to note that older horses may have more medical issues or require more maintenance than younger horses. You'll want to ensure you understand their medical history and any potential ongoing costs before making a decision. At six years old, you will have a horse that hopefully has a good foundation for you to build upon, whereas a sixteen-year-old horse will know a lot more about life but may be starting to require a little extra medical care to keep in regular work.

Male or Female?

When purchasing your first horse, one of the biggest decisions you'll need to make is whether to get a female horse (mare) or a male horse (gelding or stallion). Here are some things to consider before making your decision.

Care Needs: Male/Female

There are some differences in the care needs of male and female horses. For example, male horses will require regular cleaning of their sheath to remove the accumulation of dirt and smegma. This process is known as "cleaning the beans" and needs to be done periodically to ensure their comfort and health. Mares and stallions can also become aggressive during the breeding season, which can pose a risk to their handlers, whereas geldings are usually calmer unless there is a more complex issue present (for example, if the gelding is a is proud-cut, meaning it has been castrated but all or a part of the testis remains, or has any leftover hormones post-castration).

Once, while working with a gelding, he was acting particularly irritable and aggressive. I started checking him from nose to tail to determine if the irritability stemmed from a physical issue, and in the process I discovered that he had a bean in his sheath that was causing him discomfort. After cleaning it out, he was much happier and easier to work with. You should check for beans on a regular basis, but make sure you condition your horse to accept it. Doing this without proper acclimation to the process is a good way to get kicked. Pro tip – there is a strong unpleasant order, so you might want to use gloves.

On the other hand, mares have their own set of unique care needs. Female horses go through hormonal cycles that can cause mood swings, irritability, and even aggression. If you plan to breed your mare, you'll need to consider her reproductive health and monitor her cycles carefully. In general, in my experience (and anecdotally from dozens of other horse owners I have known over the years) mares are just generally more territorial and dominant then geldings. It is possible to spay a mare, and I have heard of this practice evening out the temperament of mares, similar to the experience of dog and cat owners.

In general, while it's important to remember that every horse is an individual and may not conform to gender stereotypes, there are some general temperament differences between male and female horses. Mares can be more opinionated and stubborn, while geldings tend to be more laid-back and easy-going. Stallions can be unpredictable and aggressive and require a more experienced handler.

One or More?

As a first-time horse buyer, you might be wondering whether you should get just one horse or more than one. Or, maybe you never thought out it at all. It's important to know that horses are social animals and thrive in a herd environment. So, if possible, it's recommended that you have more than one horse.

Socialization is a crucial aspect of owning a horse. It's not just about keeping them healthy and happy, but it's also about training them to be around other animals, people, and objects without getting anxious or scared. Horses are social animals, and they thrive in the company of their own kind. So, it's essential to provide them with enough opportunities to interact with other horses. However, if you can only have one horse don't worry, there are other options.

One option is to get a companion animal, such as a goat. Goats can make excellent pasture companions for horses, and they can also provide some entertainment and companionship for you as well. In most cases, horses and goats get along well together.

If you are at the end of your horse-y journey and don't want to get another horse, getting a goat can be a great way to keep your remaining horse company. Goats are relatively low-maintenance and can be a fun addition to your farm or stable. Plus, they have the added benefit of being able to eat some of the weeds that horses won't touch.

If you can afford it or don't have the space at home, boarding your horse at a local facility can also be a good way for your horse to socialize. This way you only need one horse of your own.

In addition to other horses, horses should also be exposed to other animals such as dogs, cats, goats, and chickens. This exposure will help them get used to the sights, sounds, and smells of different animals, and it will prevent them from getting scared or anxious when they encounter them. Socializing your horse will help them develop a calm and confident personality and reduce the likelihood of behavioral issues.

It's also crucial to socialize your horse with people. They should be comfortable being handled by humans and should be trained to behave appropriately around people. This training includes teaching them to stand still when being groomed, clipped, or trimmed/shod and to load and unload from trailers safely.

Socialization should start early on in your horse's life and should continue throughout their lifetime. It's an ongoing process that requires patience and consistency. You can use different methods to socialize your horse, including turnout with other horses, groundwork, and exposure to different environments. Every new experience will make you horse more well-adjusted to life in general.

In the end, the decision of whether to get one or more than one horse is up to you and your circumstances. Just remember that horses are social animals and thrive in a herd environment, so if possible, it's best to provide them with some companionship. And if you can't get another horse, a goat can be a great alternative.

Cost

When it comes to buying a horse, there are various factors that you need to consider, and cost is definitely one of them. Let's explore some of the cost-related aspects to help you make an informed decision.

- **Amount of Training**: One of the main factors that can impact the cost of owning a horse is the amount of training it has received. A well-trained horse will cost significantly more than a "green", or untrained horse, when you buy it. However, if you have a good trainer, you may consider getting a less-trained horse and training it yourself.
- **Size**: The size of the horse can also impact its cost, though to a much lesser extent than its level of training. Generally, larger horses cost more to feed than smaller ones. However, keep in mind that bigger horses may be more suitable for certain disciplines, such as jumping or dressage.
- **Bloodlines:** Obviously, horses with proven bloodlines (meaning their parents, grandparents, and so on have a history of high performance in whatever discipline they compete in) are more expensive to purchase than other horses.
- **Color:** Not surprisingly a horse's appearance, and particularly its color will most likely impact its cost. Some people could care less what color their horse is if it checks all the other boxes: training, temperament, breeding, etc. But, in general, a flashy paint horse and a flea-bitten grey with a multicolor mane will cost more than a "plain" sorrel horse, all other things being equal. Don't get me wrong, many

people love a sorrel horse but in general, colors that are considered more exotic will cost more.

- **Tack and Equipment Needed**: Another cost to consider when buying a horse is the tack and equipment needed. Saddles, bridles, grooming supplies, and other equipment can add up quickly. Make sure to factor in the cost of these items when considering your budget for buying a horse. Remember to look at second hand stores, auctions or online sales – you can often find good equipment this way at a much cheaper price point.
- **Maintenance Cost**: Owning a horse comes with various maintenance costs, such as feed, bedding, farrier and veterinarian services, and other miscellaneous expenses. It is essential to have a realistic understanding of these expenses before buying a horse. Depending on where you live and the services you need, these costs can vary significantly. Do your research!

Stabling

When it comes to stabling your horse, there are a few things to keep in mind. You want to make sure your horse has a safe, clean, and comfortable place to stay, whether that's a stall, a run-in shed, or a pasture.

Stalls provide the most protection and allow for more control over your horse's environment, but they also require more maintenance and can be more expensive. Run-in sheds are a good option for horses that spend a lot of time outside, and pastures are ideal for horses that need to move around and graze freely.

When selecting a stable or boarding facility, make sure to consider the location, amenities, and services offered. Look for a facility that provides clean, well-ventilated stalls or sheds, adequate turnout, and a safe environment. Make sure there is enough space for your horse to move around comfortably and get the exercise it needs.

Don't forget to factor in the cost of stabling or boarding when considering the overall cost of horse ownership if do not have your own pasture. Depending on your location and the type of facility you choose, stabling costs can vary widely. But remember, providing your horse with a safe and comfortable place to stay is an important part of being a responsible horse owner.

Where to Purchase a Horse

If you are reading this book because you are considering buying a horse, chances are you have already looked into your horse-purchasing options (or, maybe you jumped in head first and already bought one!) But, if you want more advice, here are some opportunities to consider.

Private Individuals

One option is to buy from a private individual who is selling their personal horse. This can be a good way to find a horse that has been well-cared for and has a known history. You can find private sellers through online classifieds or by networking with local horse owners.

Internet

The internet can be a great resource for finding horses for sale, but it's important to be careful when making a purchase sight unseen. Look for reputable websites and sellers with good reviews, and be prepared to ask a lot of questions and request additional photos and videos. Consider having a pre-purchase vet check done before committing to a purchase. I personally never purchase a horse without an in-person visit.

Reputable Breeders

If you have a specific breed in mind, a reputable breeder can be a good source for finding a well-bred horse with a known pedigree. Look for breeders who prioritize the health and temperament of their horses, and ask for references from previous buyers.

Horse Auctions

Auctions can be a good place to find a bargain, but they can also be risky depending on what kind of auction you attend. Horses may be sold "as is" with no guarantees, and it can be difficult to fully evaluate a horse's health and temperament in a chaotic auction environment. If you are considering buying at an auction, do your research beforehand and be prepared to set a strict budget and stick to it. There are many auctions that will allow you to visit a horse before the auction, so look into that option if you're considering purchasing a horse at an auction.

Horse Dealers

Horse dealers buy and sell horses as a business and can be a good source for finding a variety of horses at different price points. However, it's important to be careful when dealing with a dealer, as some may not have the horse's best interests at heart. Look for dealers with good reputations and ask for references from previous buyers. Let's just say the term "horse trader" came about for a reason.

Horse Rescues

You can also look for horses that are up for adoption in your area. Generally, these horses require a more experienced owner and often times are not suitable for riding as they may be older or have been mistreated or otherwise injured earlier in their life. I have personally adopted rescue horses, and I probably will again but I have had enough experience with horses to properly vet the situation and determine if I am able to take on the horse and whatever issues come with it. Be sure that you have both the time and financial where-withal to adopt a horse that may require special care if you go down this road. Rescue horses that are not suitable for riding or other activities can make great companions to your other horses, however, so keep this option in mind. Giving a rescue horse a forever home where they can live out the rest of their life as a "pasture pet" can be a very rewarding thing to do, but just be sure that you know what you are getting yourself into.

No matter where you choose to purchase your horse, always take the time to thoroughly evaluate the horse's health, temperament, and suitability for your riding goals. Don't be afraid to ask questions and seek advice from experienced horse owners and trainers. With patience and diligence, you can find the perfect horse for you.

EVALUATING PROSPECTS

When you start to visit horses you might like to purchase, it's important to evaluate your prospects carefully. Here are some tips to help you make an informed decision:

- **Consider the horse's temperament**: Look for a horse that has a good temperament and is easy to handle. If the horse is nervous or easily spooked, it may not be a good fit for a beginner rider.
- **Assess the horse's conformation**: Good conformation is essential for a horse's health and soundness. Look for a horse with straight legs, a level topline, and good muscling.
- **Evaluate the horse's movement**: When evaluating a horse's movement, look for smoothness, balance, and fluidity. A horse that moves well will be more comfortable to ride and less prone to injuries.
- **Test ride the horse**: Take the horse for a test ride to see how it responds to your cues and how it feels to ride. This will give you a good idea of the horse's training level and suitability for your riding goals.
- **Check the horse's health**: It is a good idea to have a veterinarian perform a pre-purchase exam before buying a horse, especially if you are buying a high dollar horse or you don't personally know the person selling the horse. This will help you identify any potential health

issues that may affect the horse's performance or
longevity.

- **Consider the horse's training**: If you're a beginner
  rider, look for a horse that is well-trained and
  experienced. A green or untrained horse will be
  more difficult to handle and require more training.

Remember, purchasing a horse is a big commitment and
requires careful consideration. By following these tips and
doing your research, you can ensure that you find the right
horse for your needs and goals. Additionally, some sellers
also have requirements for the home their horses go to. This
is especially true if you obtain a horse from a rescue. For
example, the Bureau of Land Management has a fairly well-
known program for the adoption of wild horses (sometimes
referred to as mustangs) and burros in the United States.
There is a lengthy list of requirements that you and your
property must meet in order to be eligible to adopt a horse
from this program, including the type and height of your
fencing and shelter requirements. While I don't necessarily
recommend adopting a horse if you are a new horse owner, I
bring this point up because sometimes even for-profit sellers
and breeders have special requirements for their prospective
customers as well and you just need to do your research.

Training Examples to Consider

Now it's time to talk about some basic training needs that
your new equine friend may require. If you are beginner, I
strongly encourage you to purchase a horse that already has
a significant amount of training. In any case, it is imperative
to review the level of training your horse will require before

you make the purchase, as correct training means spending a lot of time, effort, and potentially money on your new friend. If you take my advice and purchase a trained "been there, done that" horse, he will already have the following things down pat. However, I've included the following section on basic training needs for your horse so that you can get educated on what your horse should know. Let's get started!

- **Training to accept human touch/interaction**: If your horse is not used to being around and being touched by humans, basically no other training is possible. This may seem simplistic, and dare I say – obvious – but assuming you are a beginner, this is important to understand. Recall the multiple references to the horse as a prey animal in earlier chapters. That information is included (perhaps ad nauseum) so that you can start to understand the fundamental way a horse thinks. Fight or flight is a horse's reaction to everything unless he has been properly desensitized. Some horses, of course, are quicker to learn trust, but at their core all horses need to be properly exposed to human interaction before you have a prayer of moving forward with their training. Horses are also innately curious, so as long as their interactions with humans are positive trust can be established quickly. If your horse shies away from touch, be patient and spend time with him every day. At first you can just be there, without attempting to make contact with the horse. Then gradually move into physical touch, wherever the horse is the most comfortable. Start by introducing your horse to different types of touch, such as stroking their neck and between their eyes. Gradually work up to more intense touch, such as picking up their hooves or grooming their coat. Rubbing their ears or brushing their belly should be saved for after your horse knows you a little better and has started to trust you as these areas are often more sensitive for most horses. Eventually you should be able to touch your horse everywhere without causing anxiety. Remember to always approach your horse calmly and safely and to reward good behavior. A note about touch: people often "pat" horses; generally, horses prefer to be rubbed or scratched to being "patted".

- **Halter breaking**: One of the first things a horse learns is how to wear a halter. Many people start this training almost immediately with week-old foals. This is important for leading and handling your horse. To do this, you'll want to use a well-fitting halter and lead rope, and introduce it to your horse gradually. You can start by holding the halter up to your horse's nose and letting them sniff it. Then, you can gradually work up to putting the halter on their head and fastening it, rewarding them for good behavior. Remember to be patient and consistent, and always reward your horse for its progress. Don't force them too aggressively, or shout. If you get frustrated, your horse can feel that and your tension will create tension in the horse, and then the horse will associate the halter with tension.

- **Training to load**: At some point, you'll likely need to transport your horse, whether it's to a new location or to a vet appointment. To do this, you'll need to train your horse to load into a trailer. This can be a difficult process for some horses, but with patience and positive reinforcement, your horse can learn to load calmly and confidently.

- **Farrier** Your horse's hooves will require regular maintenance by a farrier, who is a specialist in horse hoof care. This can include trimming, shoeing, and checking for any signs of lameness or other issues. It's important to find a reliable and experienced farrier to work with, and to schedule regular appointments to keep your horse's hooves in good condition. Your horse will need to be trained to stand still for the farrier, lift his feet, and stand patiently while he is being worked on. Simply picking up your horse's feet yourself a few times a week will go a long way to training your horse to be a perfect gentleman or lady for the farrier. We'll discuss more about training to load a horse in a trailer and how to stand for the farrier in Chapter 8.

Of course, if you are completely new to the horsey world, then you will need some assistance in training your horse to be able to handle these things. Training with a professional can cost a lot of money, and finding a trainer who fits the needs of both you and your horse can take time. It is better to weigh up these points before you purchase a horse rather than struggle with them later on in your partnership.

Other Things to Consider Regarding Training Your Horse

Here are some other training aspects you should consider before purchasing your horse. Of course, these will vary depending on your skill level and access to knowledgeable trainers.

- **Walk**: Walking is the most basic gait of the horse, and it's essential that you master it before moving on to more complex gaits as a rider. Make sure to sit up straight, relax your shoulders and arms, and keep your heels down while walking. This will help you maintain your balance and communicate more effectively with the horse. Ideally, if you are new to horses then you should choose a horse who is happy to walk steadily while you are still gaining your confidence.

- **Habits of the horse when handled**: Every horse has its own personality and quirks. Some horses may be more stubborn or easily distracted than others, while some may be more sensitive or reactive to different stimuli. As a handler or rider, it's important to observe and learn about your horse's habits, so you can work with them effectively. When shopping for horses, it is better to observe these habits and assess whether they are something you are comfortable handling or not.

- **By the trainer**: A good trainer should be able to handle horses confidently and safely. They should know how to communicate effectively with the horse, use appropriate training aids, and be able to read the horse's body language to determine its mood and needs. A trainer should be able to create a positive, stress-free environment that encourages the horse to learn and improve.

- **By you**: As the rider, you also play a significant role in the horse's behavior and habits. It's important to be consistent and clear with your aids and signals, so the horse understands what you're asking for. Make sure to reward the horse when they do something right, so they associate positive outcomes with good behavior. Stay calm and patient, even if the horse is being difficult or unresponsive.

- **Responses to riding aids**: Riding aids are the signals and cues you use to communicate with the horse while riding. These can include the reins, legs, seat, and voice. It's important to learn how to use these aids effectively, so you can control the horse's movements and direction. The horse should respond promptly and willingly to your aids, but this will take practice and training. Keep in mind that different horses may respond differently to different aids, so it's important to adjust your approach as needed.

- **Other riding tips for beginners:** Here are a few things that I wished someone would have reinforced more with me when I learned to ride:

- Relax. The most important thing you can do is relax. Don't squeeze the horse with your legs, and don't be too rigid. Your horse can feel that and it's no fun for anyone. When you first start riding horses, do whatever you have to do to gain confidence. When I learned to ride, I rode every day in a fairly small fenced in area just because I was more comfortable knowing the horse couldn't go too far if I lost control.

- Don't look down. It's common for a new rider to watch the position of their hands, where the reins are, where their legs are, etc. This confuses the horse. Always look where you want the horse to go.

- Everyone says to keep your heels down. I even said it in an earlier paragraph. Yes, you need to keep your heels generally lower than your toes for balance and communication with the horse, but don't get too caught up in this. We all have different bodies, and as long as you keep your feet at least parallel with the ground, you'll be fine.

- When I saddle a horse, I tighten the girth almost all the way, and I stop. Then I put the bridle on, adjust the reins, zip up pockets, put my phone away, or whatever else I need to do before we go, and the last thing I do is tighten the girth all the way to where it needs to be. I find that this just gives the horse a moment to get used to the saddle, to the tension of the girth, and to get ready for the ride. Note: if a lot of these terms and concepts about saddling a horse are unfamiliar to you, there are a lot of videos online you can watch to learn more. The best option is to take lessons – a good instructor will take at least an entire lesson to walk you through things like the proper way to tie a horse, how to prepare a horse to be saddled, how to saddle, etc. Unfortunately reading about how to do these things in a book will only get you so far, you need to go do it!

- The best advice I ever got about learning to ride horses is to mount the horse (in other words, get on) and then stop. Make the horse stand perfectly still for a few moments before you ever move. If you do this every time you mount, the horse will not develop a tendency to start moving while you are still trying to climb into the saddle.

- My last piece of beginner's riding advice is to make small movements when you ride a new horse. Horses are extremely sensitive creatures, which is why you can often "steer" a horse just with your seat. In other words, just shifting your body weight forward slightly is enough for some horses to know that you want to move forward. No need to use the reins, your feet, your legs, or your voice. Other horses, just based on their training or their sensitivity, need more overt cues like a kick or a verbal cue to move. But whatever cue you are giving, start small. Give a soft kick, for example, and if the horse does not react, increase the intensity slightly until you get the response you are looking for. The same is true for all other cues. Start small until you learn the sensitivity of your horse. You will learn pretty quickly if your horse needs a more aggressive pull back to stop, for example.

In this chapter, you have learned about the different costs associated with owning a horse, how to evaluate a horse's potential, where to purchase a horse, and an introduction on how to train and care for a horse.

EVERYTHING HORSE FOR BEGINNERS

Now, in the next chapter, "Room to Roam," we will be discussing the importance of providing adequate space for your horse. This includes not only the size of the pasture or paddock but also the type of footing, access to water and shelter, and the number of horses per acre. By providing your horse with enough space to move and graze freely, you will help ensure their physical and mental well-being. So, let's dive into the next chapter to learn more about providing your horse with room to roam.

IF YOU ARE ENJOYING this book, please consider leaving a review. Reviews from readers like you help others identify resources for information, and when you leave a review you are supporting independent writers. My horses (pictured above) thank you in advance!

ROOM TO ROAM

> *If I paint a wild horse, you might not see the horse...*
> *but surely you will see the wildness!*

— PABLO PICASSO

In this chapter, you will better understand the space required to manage your horses. It will provide essential insights into how much space your horses need to live comfortably and safely, as well as the different types of spaces you can provide them with.

HOW MUCH SPACE DOES YOUR HORSE NEED?

When it comes to owning a horse, providing a suitable living environment is crucial for their health and happiness. The amount of space your horse needs depends on a variety of factors, including their breed, age, workload, and the natural environment where you live. In this section, we will discuss different types of living situations for horses and provide recommendations for pasture size based on these factors.

Your Own Pasture

If you have the luxury of owning your own pasture, you have the freedom to create an ideal living environment for your horse. The recommended pasture size per horse varies depending on several factors, including the breed, age, workload, and natural environment. As a general rule of thumb, it's recommended to provide at least one acre of pasture per horse. This will allow your horse to move around freely and engage in natural behaviors like grazing and socializing with other horses.

Geographical Location

The natural environment of where you live plays a significant role in determining the amount of space your horse needs. For example, if you live in an area with harsh winters, you may need to provide additional shelter and space for your horse to move around during the colder months. On the other hand, if you live in an area with mild weather year-round, your horse may not need as much shelter and space. Research what other horse owners in your do in order get a better idea of what will work best for you.

Breed or Species

Different breeds and species of horses have varying space requirements. For example, larger breeds like draft horses and warmbloods may need more space than smaller breeds like ponies and Arabians. Additionally, horses that are bred for speed and athleticism, like Thoroughbreds and Quarter Horses, may require more space to move around and stretch their muscles.

Management

Proper management is key to ensuring your horse has enough space to live a happy and healthy life. This includes regularly rotating pastures to prevent overgrazing, providing adequate shelter and access to water, and monitoring your horse's health and behavior.

Workload

Horses that are worked regularly, such as those used for riding or competition, may require more space to move around and exercise than horses that are not worked as frequently.

Age

The age of your horse can also impact the amount of space they need. Young horses, for example, may need more space to play and explore, while older horses may require more shelter and space to rest.

By taking into consideration factors like breed, age, work-load, and natural environment, you can determine the recommended pasture size per horse and create an ideal living situation for your equine companion. Remember to always prioritize proper management practices to ensure your horse has enough space to live their best life.

Stabling

Stabling is a popular option for horse owners who want to provide a safe and comfortable environment for their equine friends. If you're considering stabling your horse, there are a few important factors to consider, including freedom, friends, and forage. In this guide, we will explore why stabling can be beneficial for your horse and how you can ensure your horse has a comfortable and healthy living environment.

Freedom

One of the most important considerations when stabling your horse is providing them with enough freedom to move around and engage in natural behaviors. A well-designed stall should allow your horse to turn around, lie down, and stand up comfortably. It's also essential to provide enough space for your horse to move around and stretch their legs, which can help prevent injuries and promote good health.

Friends

Horses are social animals, and they thrive on companionship. Stabling your horse with other horses can provide them with the opportunity to socialize and interact with other animals, which can help reduce stress and improve their overall well-being. When choosing stablemates for your horse, it's important to consider their temperament and personality to ensure they will get along well.

Forage

Another important consideration when stabling your horse is ensuring they have access to enough forage. Horses are natural grazers, and they require a steady supply of hay or grass to maintain good health. When stabling your horse, make sure to provide them with enough hay or grass to last throughout the day and night. Additionally, it's essential to provide clean and fresh water at all times.

OTHER IDEAS

If you have pasture land or a horse, there are many options available to generate income while sharing your passion for horses with others. Here are some ideas to consider:

Part-Lease Your Horse

If you don't have the time or resources to care for your horse full-time, consider offering a part-lease. This option allows someone to ride and care for your horse a few days a week, while you split the costs of care.

Board Other Horses

If you have extra space on your property, consider offering boarding services to other horse owners. You can charge for the use of your pastures and stables while providing a safe and comfortable environment for other horses.

Hold Events

Hosting horse-related events on your property is a great way to generate income and bring the community together.

Consider hosting horse shows, trail rides, or other equine-related events.

Host Equine Professionals

If you have a large facility and experience in horse care, consider hosting equine professionals on your property. You can charge a fee for their use of your facility, which can include stabling, arenas, and other amenities.

Rent Your Riding Arena

If you have an indoor or outdoor riding arena, consider renting it out to local riders. You can charge a fee for use of the arena, which can help offset the costs of maintenance and care.

Offer Grazing Rights

If you have pasture land, consider offering grazing rights to other farmers or livestock owners. You can charge a fee for the use of your land while providing a valuable resource to others.

Re-Sell Hay

If you grow your own hay, you can sell the excess to other horse owners in the area. This can be a great way to generate income while helping other horse owners feed their animals.

Sell Manure

If you have horses, you have manure. Consider selling the excess to local farmers or gardeners, who may be interested in using it as fertilizer for their crops.

Provide Bed and Bale or Horse Camping Options

If you have extra space on your property, consider offering bed and bale or horse camping options for travelers passing through the area. You can charge a fee for the use of your land and facilities while providing a unique and enjoyable experience for your guests.

Offer Equine-Related Custom or Repair Services

If you have experience in equine-related custom or repair services, consider offering your services to others in the area. This can include custom saddles, leatherwork, or farrier services.

Host Hives or Keep Bees

If you have an interest in beekeeping, consider hosting hives on your property. You can sell honey or beeswax products to generate income.

Rent Storage Space

If you have unused farm buildings or storage space, consider renting it out to others in the area. This can include storage for boats, RVs, or other equipment.

Teach Art Classes

If you have a passion for art and horses, consider teaching art classes on your property. You can charge a fee for the classes and provide a unique and enjoyable experience for your students.

Teach or Offer Agricultural Skills

If you have experience in agriculture or farming, consider teaching others in the community. This can include classes on gardening, livestock care, or farm management.

Offer Boarding Services for Small Pets

If you have space available and are looking for ways to earn extra income, consider offering boarding services for small pets. This could include cats, dogs, rabbits, and other small animals. You could set up a small pet hotel on your property, complete with individual kennels or cages, bedding, toys, and even a small play area. Make sure to follow all local laws and regulations regarding pet boarding and care, and take care to provide a safe and comfortable environment for your furry guests.

Grow and Sell Extra Produce

If you have a green thumb and enjoy gardening, consider growing and selling extra produce as a way to generate additional income. You could sell your produce at local farmers' markets, set up a roadside stand, or even offer a delivery service to local customers. Some popular crops to consider growing include tomatoes, peppers, cucumbers, zucchini, and herbs. Consider offering a variety of options, including organic or heirloom varieties, to appeal to a wider customer base.

As you can see, there are many different ways to generate extra income from your horse property. Whether you choose to offer boarding services, rent out space, or explore other creative options, the key is to think outside the box and find ways to maximize the potential of your property. By doing so, you can not only earn extra income but also make the most of your land and resources while providing valuable services and experiences for others.

FENCING

As a horse owner, one of your top priorities is the safety of your equine friend. This is especially important when it comes to your horse's fencing. Good fencing helps to keep your horse safe, secure and prevents him from wandering off into dangerous situations. Here are some tips to keep in mind when it comes to horse fence safety.

Posts: Strong and Secure

The key to a good horse-proof fence is having strong and secure posts. Posts serve as the foundation of your fencing system and will ensure that your fence is stable and reliable. You can use wooden posts, steel T-posts, pipe posts, railroad ties, or other barrier posts.

Types of Fences: Choosing the Right One

There are many types of fences available to choose from, so it's important to choose the one that is best for your needs. Here are some popular types of horse fencing:

- **Wood Board Fence**: This classic style is popular for a reason. Wood board fences are attractive, durable, and provide good visibility for horses. They require regular maintenance but are worth the effort.

- **PVC Board Fence**: This type of fence is low-maintenance, easy to clean, and comes in a variety of colors. It's also durable and can last for many years.
- **Pipe Steel Fence**: This fence is strong and durable, making it a popular choice for horse owners. It's also low-maintenance and can withstand harsh weather conditions.
- **High Tensile Wire Fence**: This fence is a cost-effective option and is easy to install. It's important to note that it's not as visible as other types of fences and can cause injury to horses if they run into it.
- **Smooth Wire Fence**: This type of fence is similar to high tensile wire, but is more visible and has a smoother surface. It's also more expensive than high-tensile wire fencing.
- **Woven Field Fence**: This fence is made of galvanized wire and is durable and strong. It's also more visible than high tensile wire fencing, making it a good choice for horses.
- **V-Mesh Fence**: This fence is similar to woven field fencing but has smaller openings. It's a good choice for horses that are prone to pawing at the fence.

Electric Fencing: An Alternative Option

Electric fencing can be a good option for horse owners who want a flexible and cost-effective fencing solution. It's important to remember that electric fencing can be dangerous if not installed correctly, so it's best to seek professional advice before installing it. I've used a lot of electric fencing over the years as I've moved horses around my property while the permanent fencing was under construction. It does its job, but I do find that wildlife, especially deer, elk and moose tear it down often which is very frustrating. If you use this option, be sure to check it regularly for this and also to ensure it has not slipped and come into contact with metal, which will cause a short and de-electrify the whole thing.

TRAINING/MENTAL STIMULATION

Whether you are keeping horses to enjoy as pets or you intend to compete in your chosen discipline, one thing for certain is that it is your responsibility to educate your horse to tolerate certain necessities. For example, your horse will definitely need to see a farrier to maintain good hoof health; therefore, as a horse owner, it is your job to build trust with your horse. Halter break them, get them used to being handled, and have their legs lifted so when the farrier does come, it is a safe and enjoyable experience for everyone involved. At some point, you will probably need to transport your horse somewhere, which means you should definitely get them comfortable loading into a horse trailer and traveling in one. By taking on a horse, you are becoming responsible for a larger flight animal, so by leaving them completely untrained, you are being extremely irresponsible and potentially opening up other people and your horse to having an accident or injury.

But it is not just training that is a part of horse ownership; you should also consider mental stimulation for your horse. This can come in a variety of different forms, but the most important thing is that your horse is happy and interested in the form you choose.

Invest in Indoor and Outdoor Toys

Keeping your horse mentally stimulated is crucial for their overall health and happiness. Investing in some indoor and outdoor toys can be an excellent way to keep your horse entertained and prevent boredom.

Horsemen's Jolly Ball

The Horsemen's Jolly Ball is a popular toy that horses love to play with. This large ball comes in different sizes and colors and can withstand rough play. Your horse will love kicking, chasing, and rolling this ball around.

Traffic Cones

You can use traffic cones to create obstacles and courses for your horse to navigate through. It's a fun way to teach your horse new skills, improve their agility and coordination, and build their confidence.

Inflatable Horse Ball

Another fun option is the inflatable horse ball, which is similar to the Jolly Ball. This ball comes in different sizes and colors and is perfect for horses who love to play.

Salt on a Rope

Salt on a rope is an excellent way to provide your horse with a healthy treat while also keeping them mentally stimulated. Your horse will enjoy licking the salt and trying to reach it as it swings back and forth.

30-Gallon Plastic Water Barrel

A 30-gallon plastic water barrel can be a great toy for horses who like to play with water. You can fill the barrel with water and let your horse splash around, which can be a fun way to cool off during the hot summer months.

Build a Slow-Feeding Hay Dispenser

Building a slow-feeding hay dispenser can be an excellent way to provide your horse with a steady supply of hay while also keeping them mentally stimulated. This type of dispenser slows down your horse's eating habits, which can improve their digestion and reduce the risk of colic.

Teach Them a New Discipline

Teaching your horse a new discipline, such as dressage, jumping, roping, or trail riding, can be an exciting and challenging experience for both you and your horse. It's an excellent way to improve your horse's physical and mental abilities and deepen your bond with them.

Switch Up Their Routine

Horses thrive on routine, but it's also important to switch things up occasionally to keep them mentally stimulated. Try taking a different route during your trail rides, changing their feeding schedule, or introducing new toys or obstacles to their environment.

Set Aside Time to Interact and Play

Setting aside time to interact and play with your horse can be an excellent way to deepen your bond and keep them mentally stimulated. You can play games, teach them new tricks, or simply spend time grooming and bonding with them.

IN THIS CHAPTER, you have learned about the importance of a horse's environment, stabling, the various options available for boarding and earning income from your horse property, different types of fencing, and how to keep your horse mentally stimulated and well-trained.

In the next chapter, we will dive deeper into the inner workings of a horse's brain, including their cognitive abilities, emotions, and social behavior. Understanding how horses think and feel will help you better communicate with them.

INSIDE THE MIND OF A HORSE

> *A horse doesn't care how much you know until he knows how much you care.*

— PAT PIRELLI

U nderstanding how a horse thinks and reacts to different stimuli is key to building a successful relationship with your equine friend. In this chapter, we will explore the science behind horse behavior and how you can use this knowledge to enhance your interactions with your horse. From instinctive behaviors to learning processes, we will cover it all. So, buckle up and get ready to explore the amazing world of a horse's mind.

HOW A HORSE'S BRAIN WORKS

As a horse owner, understanding how your horse's brain works is essential to having a good relationship with them. A horse's behavior is rooted in its prey instincts, and understanding this will allow you to communicate with them more effectively.

What Horses and Humans See

To better understand a horse's behavior, it's important to compare and contrast how they see the world versus how humans see it. Horses have a wider range of vision than humans, but they have blind spots directly in front and behind them. They also have a better ability to see movement than humans do, which is why they can spook easily if something suddenly moves. (Recall my story about my horses reacting to me moving inside my house from a few football fields away.) Understanding how horses perceive the world around them will help you train and interact with them more effectively and reduce frustration for both of you.

Bonding With Your Horse

Bonding with your horse is a crucial part of building a good relationship with them. The key is to get your horse to no longer see you as a threat and to see you as a trusted companion instead. This can be achieved through spending time with them, grooming them, and simply being in their presence. Remember that horses have long memories, so one negative interaction can undo a lot of progress. Each horse is different, but these basic concepts apply to all horses in some capacity.

Some horses, especially older ones with more experience, may act differently from inexperienced horses. They may be more confident around people and more at ease in different environments. Understanding how each individual horse responds to different situations will help you tailor your training and interactions to best suit their personality.

Horses Are Curious Creatures

Horses are curious about everything around them. They are always investigating new things and exploring their surroundings, even when they end up spooking themselves in the process. In fact, it's crucial to nurture their natural curiosity to keep them engaged and happy. Horses are natural explorers, and you can encourage their curiosity by introducing them to new experiences gradually. You can also provide them with toys and puzzles that stimulate their minds and help them learn.

Horses in the Wild

Horses have fascinating behavior in the wild, where they live in herds and rely on their instincts to survive. Observing horses in their natural habitat can give us insights into their behavior and help us understand them better. Horses in their natural habitats have a complex social herd and often live alongside members of their own family for life. They rely on communication and body language to interact with each other and form strong bonds.

Monty Roberts on Horses in the Wild

Monty Roberts is a famous horse trainer and behaviorist who has studied wild horses extensively. He has observed that wild horses have a sophisticated social structure and rely on non-verbal communication to interact with each other. In an article by the Baltimore Sun, Roberts explains that wild horses are highly attuned to each other's body language and use it to communicate their intentions and emotions (Baltimore sun, 1997). Understanding their language can help us build a stronger bond with our domesticated horses.

Horses Around Other Horses

Horses are social animals that thrive on companionship, not only for their general happiness but for survival in the wild. They communicate with each other using a complex language that is difficult for humans to understand without proper study and observation. Horses form strong bonds with their companions  and rely on them for social interaction, comfort, and protection.

Charlie stands guard while the other horses nap

Horses are happier and less stressed when they have other horses around them. If you have a single horse, it's essential to provide them with companionship, either by introducing a second horse or by allowing them to interact with other horses.

COMMUNICATION STRATEGY

You already know that when you are developing a relationship with a horse it is important to build a strong and trusting bond. For years, one tried and true way that horsemen and women have been starting this bond with horses is to get them moving. The way into a horse's head is often through his feet, as the saying goes. You need to get him moving to start real communication with him. The concept is taught by many different professional trainers today, but the underlying concepts have been used by horsemen and women for a very long time and can help you establish a deep connection with your horse. In this section, we'll dive into how to work this strategy, its benefits, and how it can help you build trust with your equine partner.

Understanding Horse Communication

First and foremost, remember (I know, again) that horses are prey animals. In the wild, they rely on their herd for protection and survival. As a result, they are wired to be constantly aware of their surroundings and to always be on the lookout for danger. When you approach a horse, they see you as a potential predator until proven otherwise.

This is where effective communication comes in. It's essential to communicate with your horse in a way that makes sense to <u>him</u>. Building a relationship with your horse based on trust and mutual respect is the most effective way to train a horse. You should train your horse, and communicate with your horse in a way that makes them see you as a leader. When done correctly, this type of approach to training can create a deep sense of trust between you and your horse, which can lead to better performance, less anxiety, and a stronger bond.

Establishing Trust and Respect Through Movement and Physical Cues

This process involves a series of steps that you'll need to follow in order to establish trust with your horse. Several expert horse trainers have their own approach to similar processes, but the description below is the strategy that has worked well for me. You can also watch videos online on how to perform similar training sessions with your horse. I highly recommend Monty Roberts. To do this exercise, you will need: a circular pen/corral (often referred to as a round pen), that is about 50 feet across and a halter and lead rope.

Step 1: **Push Your Horse Around A Round Pen**

This doesn't mean literally to physically push your horse. "Pushing" refers to taking actions to make your horse run around the perimeter of the pen.

Lead your horse into the pen, relaxed, and shut the gate. Move to the center of the pen. You can turn your horse to face different angles in the pen while remaining in the center to acclimate him to the pen, and give him a rub between the eyes. Disconnect the lead rope, and move away from the horse. Then, signal the horse to move away from you by waving your hands or smacking the lead rope against your pant leg. Make eye contact with the horse. Square your shoulders up to the horse as well, all at the same time. Direct eye contact, squaring up, and waving your arm with an open hand are all signals that mean "Move away from me!" in horse-speak. Your demeanor should be confident and projecting the fact that you are in a leadership role, you are in charge, and that you want the horse to move away from you, but it should not be threatening, or angry, or nervous. You should, however project high, confident energy. You will stay towards the middle of the pen with the horse running the perimeter. Your extended, waving arm should be the arm positioned "behind" the horse, so that it is pushing him forward the way you want him to go. Keep the horse moving around the outside of the pen in the same direction at a lope or slow gallop for at least 4 or 5 laps. Do not let him stop or turn around. If he starts to slow or tries to turn around, move towards him with your shoulders square to him and wave your arms. He needs to go where you are telling him to go. You can also toss one end of the rope towards the horse's hind quarters to get him to move; the rope does not even have to touch him, but it can. You aren't "whipping" the horse, you are simply tossing the end of the rope in his general direction. (I always send the horse to my right first, but I don't think it really matters which way to send the horse to start.)

Step 2: Change Directions

Once your horse has made 4 to 5 laps, you want to cause him to change directions and run the opposite direction around the round pen for another 4 to 5 laps. To do this, quickly move slightly into the horse's path while still remaining safely in the middle of the pen, drop your arm and lift the other arm in the air, with an open palm, and wave your hand. This will be the hand/arm positioned near the front of the horse until he turns. Most horses turn easily when you do this, but some will be slower to stop and turn; never jump directly into his path, but move that direction so he knows you want him to go the other way. Continue your "move away from me" posture and energy, with square shoulders, direct eye contact, and an extended arm with an open palm and push him around the pen in this new direction for 4 to 5 laps.

Step 3: Change Directions a Second Time.

Change your horse's direction again so he is running in the original direction you started from, and start the circles again. After one circle, you can lower your energy. Keep him moving, but it can be at a less intense pace. Your horse should begin to slow his movement as well as your energy lowers.

Step 4: Watch for the Horse to Communicate with You

At this point the horse should start to communicate back to you. He may even have started some of these communications before you got to the third stage of the circle. Every horse is a little different at when, and in what order they will do these four things, but you are looking for him to: 1) point his inside ear toward you and not move it away; this means you have his attention and respect, 2) look over at you and start making smaller circles in the pen, he will keep moving but move off of the perimeter and closer to the center; this means he wants to come closer to you, 3) lick and chew; this means he has lower adrenaline and he is signaling to you that he is not a threat and is considering that you are not a threat either, and 4) lower his head; this signals that he is looking for a leader, and that leader is you!

Step 5: Allow Your Horse to Slow and Approach You

When, and only when, the horse exhibits all four of these communications to you, you can let him stop moving around the pen. I like to make sure the horse has a lot of "heads down" posturing before I let him stop moving. If he has not yet exhibited all four of these communications, I send the horse the other direction again and keep my energy up until I see all four things that I am looking for. Once you are ready to signal to your horse that he can stop moving around the pen, close your hand and lower your arm to your side. Also lower your energy. Allow the horse to stop and look at you. Take a small step away from him, turn your shoulders at a 45-degree angle to his face, and remove eye contact. These actions all signal to him that you will now allow him to approach you. Your horse may move toward you at this point, and if he does not, starting taking small steps away from him. If he still does not follow up, and he looks away, advance toward him. Retreat when he looks at you. (Advance and retreat is a common phrase used by horsemen). Once he follows you continuously, walk around for a bit and let him follow you. Finally stop, turn towards him still avoiding eye contact and rub him between the eyes. Walk away again, and he should follow you. Continue to stop, rub between the eyes, walk away, and repeat. Reverse directions. He should continue to follow up. Getting your horse to follow you at the end of the exercise is the goal of this activity. When he follows you, he is communicating to you that he trusts you and sees you as a leader.

Benefits of This Communication to Establish Trust

The purpose of this exercise is to communicate to your horse that you are his leader, he can trust you, and you know how to communicate with him. I always do this with new horses when they come to live on my farm. This is a very good way for a horse to get to know you and understand their place in the "herd order", where you are the leader. Again, horses look for and will follow a good leader. You need to establish yourself as that leader. This strategy gives you a way to do that in the horse's own language. It is based on how horses interact and communicate with each other, which is why I believe it is so effective. This technique has never failed for me – but it can be more challenging with horses with aggression or other behavioral issues. If you find yourself in a situation like that, you should seek the advice of a professional trainer.

There are many benefits of establishing this greater trust and understanding with your horse:

- **Stronger Bond**: These kinds of exercises can help you establish a deeper, more meaningful bond with your horse.
- **Improved Performance**: When your horse trusts and respects you, they'll be more willing to perform and work with you.
- **Reduced Anxiety**: Horses that have a strong bond with their handlers are often less anxious and more relaxed.

The specific strategy I described above should only be done with the same horse a handful of times; that is all that it takes for the lessons to be ingrained in him. If you do this exercise with a horse too many times, he will get bored. A bored horse will eventually become a frustrated horse. From here, you can move on to more advanced training.

In conclusion, this strategy of using movement and horse-speak is a powerful training technique that can help you establish trust and respect with your horse. By following the steps outlined above, you can create a deep and meaningful bond with your equine partner that will last a lifetime.

As prey animals, horses are naturally wary of humans, but using horse-speak as a training technique, we can communicate with them in a way that makes them see us as a leader and not a predator. By following the steps outlined in the chapter, you can create a deep and meaningful bond with your horse, which can lead to improved performance, reduced anxiety, and a stronger connection.

IN THE NEXT CHAPTER, we'll dive even deeper into the emotional bond between horses and their owners. We'll explore the science behind this bond and how it can impact both the horse and the human. You'll learn about the role of oxytocin, the hormone responsible for social bonding, and how it can be triggered through positive interactions with your horse. By the end of the next chapter, you'll have a better understanding of the emotional connection between horses and their owners and how you can strengthen this bond with your own equine partner.

THE LANGUAGE OF A HORSE

> His mane was like a crest, mounting, then falling low. His neck was long and slender, and arched to the small, savagely beautiful head. The head was that of the wildest of all wild creatures- a stallion born wild- and it was beautiful, savage, splendid. A stallion with a wonderful physical perfection that matched his savage, ruthless spirit.
>
> — WALTER FARLEY

As social animals, horses have evolved to read and respond to the emotions of those around them, including humans. In turn, our own emotions can have a profound impact on our horses, influencing their behavior and even their physical health. Understanding the science behind this emotional connection can help us build a stronger bond with our horses, leading to a more rewarding and fulfilling relationship. So, in this chapter, we'll dive into the fascinating world of equine emotions and explore how we can use this knowledge to enhance our interactions with our equine partners.

UNDERSTANDING THE EMOTIONS OF YOUR HORSE—READING THEIR BODY LANGUAGE

As you prepare to ride your horse, it's important to understand their emotions and how they communicate them through body language. Taking the time to build a relationship with your horse before attempting to mount them is important to get the performance you are looking for from your horse.

How Emotion Influences Horse and Rider Behavior

Horses are highly attuned to the emotions of their riders and reflect these emotions in their behavior. If you're feeling anxious or stressed, your horse may become more skittish or nervous, while a calm and relaxed rider can help to keep their horse calm and relaxed. This interplay between horse and rider emotions is supported by research, which has found that horses are emotional sponges that pick up on the emotions of those around them (Lesté-Lasserre, MA, 2020). But frankly, once you spend enough time around horses, you don't need any formal research to tell you that.

Before we delve into how to read your horse's state of mind, it's essential to emphasize the importance of building a relationship with your horse. By spending time with your horse on the ground, grooming them, and engaging in groundwork exercises, you can begin to develop a deeper understanding of their personality and body language. This bond of trust and mutual respect can translate into a more successful and enjoyable riding experience.

Reading Your Horse's Body Language

Horses are highly attuned to body language and non-verbal cues, and they communicate their emotions through subtle changes in their behavior and movements. By learning to recognize and interpret these cues, you can gain insight into your horse's mood and respond accordingly. Some common signs of a horse's emotions include:

- **Ears**: Horses' ears can indicate their level of attention or alertness. If your horse's ears are turned back, it could mean they are annoyed, frustrated, or in pain. However, it's important to distinguish between ears that are simply turned back and those that are flat and pinned against the horse's head. Flat ears that are pinned suggest that the horse is more than just annoyed or frustrated; they are either fearful or angry. It's also worth noting that a horse's eyes follow the movement of its ears, so when its ears are turned back, they are likely looking in that direction with the corresponding eye.

Whiskey has one ear pointed back, one ear forward to watch both in front and behind while he works cattle

- Ears that are pricked and facing forward often indicate excitement or that something has grabbed the attention of your horse. Understanding these subtleties in a horse's body language can help you better communicate with and care for your equine friend.

- **Eyes**: A horse's eyes can convey a range of emotions, from calm to anxious or fearful. Widened eyes with whites showing indicate fear or anxiety, while a soft, relaxed eye indicates calmness.

- **Body posture**: Horses' body language can also reveal their emotions. A relaxed, loose posture indicates calmness, while a tense, stiff posture may indicate anxiety or fear.

HOW HORSES UNDERSTAND HUMAN EMOTIONS

Many people describe their horse as their best friend, therapist, or favorite companion. But how do horses really understand human emotions? In this chapter, we'll explore the unique bond between horses and humans and how horses are able to accurately and fairly interpret our emotions.

The Unique Bond between Horses and Humans

Horses have been domesticated for thousands of years and have played an important role in human history and culture. They've been used for transportation, agriculture, and warfare and have also served as loyal companions and sources of entertainment. This long history of human-horse interaction has created a unique bond between the two species.

According to research, horses are able to recognize individual human faces and voices and can distinguish between human emotions (Davis, 2014). This ability is thought to be due to the social and communicative nature of horses in the wild, where they rely on visual and auditory cues to communicate with other members of their herd.

How Horses Read Human Emotions

Horses are highly attuned to human body language and vocal cues and can interpret these cues to understand our emotions. For example, a horse may become nervous or agitated if they sense that their rider is anxious or tense. On the other hand, a calm and relaxed rider can help to keep their horse calm and relaxed. Horses can also sense when your heartbeat increases or decreases, and will interpret this as you being more or less anxious or alert.

Research has also found that horses are able to interpret human facial expressions and can distinguish between different emotions, such as happiness, anger, and fear. This ability is thought to be due to the similarities between human and equine facial expressions, such as the position of the eyebrows and mouth (Davis, 2014).

The Role of Trust in Human-Horse Relationships

Trust is an essential component of any human-horse relationship. Horses are prey animals, and they rely on trust and cooperation to survive in the wild. By building a relationship of trust and mutual respect with your horse, you can create a foundation for a strong and meaningful partnership.

One way to build trust with your horse is through consistent and fair training methods that focus on positive reinforcement rather than punishment. This approach can help to foster a sense of trust and cooperation between you and your horse, which can lead to a more enjoyable and successful riding experience.

HORSE PERSONALITIES

Just like humans, horses have unique personalities that distinguish them from each other. Recognizing the different personalities of horses can help people provide the best care and handling for their horses. In this section, we will explore the main types of horse personalities and how to identify them.

Social Horses

Social horses are friendly and outgoing, and they love to be around people and other horses. They are easy to handle and often make great companions for riders. They thrive in a group setting and love to be the center of attention. Social horses are often more receptive to training because they enjoy interacting with their owners.

EVERYTHING HORSE FOR BEGINNERS

Aloof Horses

Aloof horses are the opposite of social horses. They are independent and often keep to themselves. They are not as outgoing or friendly and may require more patience and time to build trust. Aloof horses may need more one-on-one attention to develop a bond with their owners. They may not enjoy being around other horses or people as much as social horses.

Fearful Horses

Fearful horses are nervous and easily spooked. They usually have had a bad experience in the past that causes them to be anxious around people or in certain situations. Fearful horses require a gentle approach to build trust and may need extra training to help them overcome their fears. They require a calm and patient handler who can help them feel secure.

Challenging Horses

Challenging horses are dominant and may try to test their owner's authority. They can be stubborn and difficult to handle, but they are often very intelligent and quick learners. Challenging horses require a confident and experienced handler who can establish clear boundaries and maintain control.

Understanding horse personalities can help you tailor their training and care to meet their specific needs. Every horse is unique, and understanding their personality can help you develop a deeper connection with them.

HORSE TEMPERAMENT

Understanding the temperament of your horse is another crucial element for creating a harmonious and productive relationship.

Quiet Horses

Quiet horses are serene, laid-back, and easy to handle. They are usually very patient, which makes them ideal for beginner riders and children. They are not easily spooked and tend to remain calm in stressful situations. They are great for leisurely riding and can be perfect for a calming trail ride.

Interested Horses

Interested horses are curious, alert, and inquisitive.

They enjoy learning new things and are always eager to try something different. They are highly intelligent and can become bored easily if they are not challenged. They are great for training, and their curiosity can be harnessed to teach them new skills.

Nervous Horses

Nervous horses are easily frightened and can be challenging to handle. They tend to be highly sensitive to their surroundings and can become easily spooked by sudden noises or movements. They require a calm and patient rider who can help them overcome their fears. Nervous horses can be excellent competition horses, but they require a lot of training and patience.

Extremely Nervous Horses

Extremely nervous horses are highly reactive and can be dangerous to handle. They are easily frightened, and their reactions can be unpredictable. They require an experienced rider who can work with them patiently and consistently to overcome their fears. Extremely nervous horses are not suitable for all riders.

Stubborn Horses

Stubborn horses can be difficult to handle, as they have a strong will and are not easily persuaded. They require a confident and assertive rider who can provide clear guidance and boundaries. Stubborn horses can be great for competition, as their determination can be harnessed to achieve great results.

Treacherous Horses

Treacherous horses are dangerous and unpredictable, with a tendency to lash out and bite or kick. They require an experienced trainer who can work with them safely and patiently. Treacherous horses are not suitable for most riders, and safety should always be the top priority.

Understanding your horse's temperament is key to building a productive and enjoyable relationship. Knowing your horse's personality and traits can help you choose the right handling and training techniques and create a comfortable and harmonious environment for both you and your horse.

THE HORSE'S INTERPRETATION OF HUMAN BODY LANGUAGE

As prey animals, horses rely heavily on their instinctive ability to read body language, and the way we communicate with our horses through our body language can make or break the relationship we have with them.

Vocal Communication

While horses are not vocal animals, they do respond to human vocal communication. Your tone of voice can have a significant impact on how your horse responds to you. Horses are very sensitive to high-pitched and loud noises, which can cause them to become nervous or frightened. In contrast, a calm and soothing voice can help to calm your horse and reassure them.

Physical Communication

Horses use their body language to communicate with one another, and they are also very good at reading human body language. The way we stand, move, and position our bodies can convey a lot of information to our horses. As discussed in the earlier discussion about pushing your horse around a round pen, an open hand with fingers extended and arm up simulates predator activity, whereas a closed hand with the arm down signifies that you are not a predator. Similarly, direct eye contact can be interpreted by horses as a sign of aggression, so it's best to avoid staring at your horse unless you are doing it intentionally to elicit an appropriate response.

Dominant or Submissive Natures of Humans

Horses have a keen ability to sense whether a human is dominant or submissive in nature, and they will respond accordingly. For instance, if you are hesitant or lack confidence, your horse may interpret this as a sign of weakness and may become nervous or anxious or will simply not respond to your instructions. On the other hand, if you are confident and assertive, your horse will be more likely to respond positively to your commands. I once had an awesome horse named Whiskey, early in my horse-owning time, that was definitely a "been there done that" horse. He was dead broke to ride and an excellent ranch horse. He was great with me on the ground, loved to be groomed, was great around kids, and stood like a champ at the mounting block for me (for those readers that don't know, a mounting block is a set of two or three stairs that a rider and use to mount a horse.) However, he definitely knew that I was a beginner rider. I could sit on his back and kick as hard as I could, and he would not move. He knew that I did not know how to make him move. My husband, however, who has been riding since he was a child jumped on Whiskey and could take off with no problems. My husband roped calves on Whiskey, drug them to the branding fire, the whole nine yards. But for me, he wouldn't even walk around the corral because he just didn't want to and he knew I didn't know how to make him do it. I had to gain a lot confidence and assert myself as the dominant partner in the relationship, which I did purely with attitude once I figured it out. No amount of physical force from me was going to work with him.

Body Language in Horse and Human Interactions

The way we approach a horse and interact with them can have a significant impact on the relationship we have with them. For example, if you approach a horse with your shoulders hunched and your body tense, they may interpret this as a sign of aggression or fear, and they will be less likely to trust you. By contrast, if you approach a horse with your shoulders back and your body relaxed, they will be more likely to see you as a friend and ally.

Eye Contact

Eye contact can be a tricky subject when it comes to horses. While horses do rely on visual cues to interpret the world around them, as mentioned before direct eye contact can be seen as a sign of aggression. Instead of staring at your horse, try to look at them with a soft gaze and avoid prolonged eye contact.

By understanding how horses interpret human body language, you can improve your communication with your horse and build a stronger bond. By being aware of your own body language and vocal cues, you can communicate more effectively with your horse and establish a relationship based on trust and respect.

UNDERSTANDING THE BODY LANGUAGE OF YOUR HORSE

Horses can communicate with humans through their body language, and understanding their nonverbal cues is essential to building a strong bond between you and your horse. Here are some common body language cues to watch for:

Head Carriage

- Lowered head: Your horse may lower their head when they're relaxed and content, eating or sleeping.
- Elevated head: An elevated head could mean your horse is excited, curious, or alert.
- Snaking: If your horse is snaking its head and neck, it could indicate aggression or discomfort.

Ears

- Turned out to the side: When your horse's ears are turned out to the side, it means they are relaxed and paying attention to their surroundings.
- Turned back: If your horse's ears are turned back, it usually means he is looking in that direction.
- Turned back, pinned against the horse's head: If your horse's ears are pinned, it means they are annoyed, frustrated, angry or in pain.
- Rapidly swiveling: Swiveling ears can indicate that your horse is trying to locate a sound or potential threat.

Legs

- Cocked: A cocked hind leg is usually a sign of relaxation.
- Raised: Raised hind legs can indicate that your horse is annoyed, angry, or in pain and may be preparing to strike or kick.
- Pawing: A horse paws at the ground when tied because he wants attention, is bored, or is anticipating food. Horses also often paw the ground before they roll.

Muzzle

- Drooping lip, slack mouth: This is a sign of relaxation, especially after a meal or when they're being groomed.
- Chewing: Horses often chew when they're content and relaxed. Licking and chewing can also be a sign of submission, as discussed in the round pen exercise.
- Clacking teeth: This could indicate your horse is in pain or discomfort.
- Flehman: This is when your horse curls their upper lip to bring in more scents. It's usually seen in stallions during mating season.
- Flared nostrils: Flared nostrils indicate excitement, exertion, or anxiety.
- Tight, pinched, or pursed mouth or muzzle: A tight or pursed mouth or muzzle could indicate pain, anxiety, or stress.

- Gaping mouth with visible teeth: Your horse may show its teeth when in pain or about to bite.

Eyes

- Tightening of muscles around the eyes: This could indicate stress or discomfort.
- Rapid darting: Rapid eye movements can indicate that your horse is scanning its environment for potential threats.
- Visible whites of the eyes: Known as "whites of the eyes," this could indicate fear, pain, or discomfort.
- Half-closed eyes: This indicates that your horse is relaxed, or even dozing.

Tail

- Raised or flagged: A raised or flagged tail means your horse is excited, happy, or showing off.
- Clamped down: A clamped-down tail is a sign of fear, anxiety, or aggression.

- General swishing: Your horse is most likely swapping at insects.
- Rapid swishing: A rapidly swishing tail could mean your horse is annoyed or angry.

Whole Body

- Rigid muscles, stiff movements: Stiff movements and rigid muscles could indicate your horse is in pain or uncomfortable.
- Trembling: Trembling can indicate that your horse is scared or in pain, or shivering from cold.
- Touching you: Your horse may nudge you when they're feeling affectionate or seeking attention.
- Swinging hindquarters: This could indicate discomfort or impatience.

By understanding your horse's body language, you can identify their emotional state and adjust your approach to ensure they feel comfortable and safe. Remember to always approach your horse slowly and calmly and observe their reactions to your presence. With time and patience, you can build a strong bond with your horse based on mutual trust and respect.

SOUNDS

It's important to understand the various sounds your horse makes and what they mean. Horses communicate through sounds that convey their emotions and intentions. The following resources will help you identify and interpret these sounds.

Nicker

A nicker is a low-pitched, soft sound that a horse makes by exhaling through its nose. This sound is usually an expression of happiness or contentment, and horses often use it to greet their owners.

Neigh

A neigh is a loud, high-pitched sound that horses make by exhaling through their nose and throat. This sound is a call for attention or a way to communicate with other horses. Horses also use neighs to express excitement or fear.

Grunts

Grunts are short, low-pitched sounds that horses make by exhaling through their nose. Horses often grunt when they are focused on a task, such as eating or exerting physical effort.

Snorting

Snorting is a forceful exhalation of air through the nose. Horses often snort when they are surprised or startled, as a way to clear their nasal passages, or to communicate their dominance.

Squeal

A squeal is a high-pitched, piercing sound that horses make by exhaling through their nose and throat. Horses use squeals as a warning or to express aggression towards other horses or people.

Groan

A groan is a low-pitched, prolonged sound that horses make when they are in pain or discomfort. Horses may also groan when they are feeling relaxed and content.

Sigh

A sigh is a long, deep exhalation of air through the nose and mouth. Horses often sigh when they are feeling relaxed and content.

Scream

A scream is a loud, piercing sound that horses make when they are in pain or danger. Horses also use screams as a way to communicate with other horses over long distances.

By being able to identify these sounds, you can better understand your horse's mood and needs. Remember, horses are social animals, and communication is essential to their well-being.

AGE-RELATED BEHAVIORAL CHANGES

As horses age, their behavior and temperament can change. It's important to understand these changes so that you can provide the best possible care for your equine friend. In this article, we'll discuss the behavioral differences between older horses and younger horses and how a horse's experiences shape them.

Behavioral Differences Between Older and Younger Horses

- **Energy Level**: Young horses are known for their high energy levels, whereas older horses tend to have a more relaxed temperament. Older horses are less likely to become agitated or anxious compared to their younger counterparts.
- **Physical Capabilities**: As horses age, their physical abilities decrease. Older horses may not be able to run as fast or jump as high as they once did. They may also experience joint stiffness, making it difficult for them to move around comfortably.
- **Social Behavior**: Younger horses tend to be more social and playful than older horses. Older horses often prefer the company of their familiar herd and may be less interested in interacting with other horses.

- **Response to Training**: Younger horses tend to be more receptive to training and new experiences compared to older horses. Older horses may take longer to learn new things and may require more patience and gentle encouragement.

How a Horse's Experiences Shape Them

- **Early Life Experiences**: A horse's experiences during its developmental stages shape its behavior later in life. For instance, foals that are hand-reared may be less emotional when placed in a new environment than naturally reared foals. Such foals may also show less fear of humans, making them difficult to handle as adult horses.
- **Quality of Maternal Care**: The quality of maternal care that a foal receives can influence the development of stereotypical behaviors in horses. Foals that receive proper maternal care are more likely to have a well-adjusted temperament as adult horses.
- **Handling and Training**: Handling young horses during specific developmental stages can optimize their reactivity later in life. Foals that observe their dams being handled agreeably are more likely to have a calm temperament as adult horses. Yearling horses that had been handled as sucklings also learn faster than horses that had almost no handling.

Understanding the behavioral differences between older and younger horses and how a horse's experiences shape them is crucial for providing the best possible care for your equine friend. As your horse ages, it's important to adapt your approach to training and handling to accommodate its changing temperament and physical abilities. By doing so, you'll be able to maintain a strong and fulfilling bond with your horse throughout their life.

"FIXING" ISSUES

Some issues your horse might have are possible to remedy. Let's look at some common problems you may face and some tips to help solve the problem. Remember – it is going to be your call to determine whether or not you can try to address these issues on your own, or if your horse requires a professional trainer.

Aggression: Charging, Biting, Kicking, etc.

- **Identify the Root Cause**: Aggression in horses can be caused by a variety of factors, such as fear, pain, stress, or dominance. Identifying the root cause is crucial for developing a suitable training plan.
- **Implement Positive Reinforcement**: Positive reinforcement training can help positively shape your horse's behavior. By rewarding good behavior with treats or praise, you encourage your horse to repeat it.
- **Avoid Negative Reinforcement**: Negative reinforcement, such as punishment or scolding, can worsen aggression problems in horses. It can cause

them to become more fearful or stressed, leading to more aggressive behavior.

- **Gradual Desensitization**: Gradual desensitization is a training technique that involves gradually exposing your horse to a feared stimulus, such as a saddle or trailer, tarps, plastic bags, or whatever else causes your horse to show fear, in a positive, non-threatening way. This technique can help your horse learn to tolerate the stimulus without reacting aggressively.

Head Shy/Belly Shy/"insert part of the body" Shy

- **Gentle and Patient Training**: Start by building trust with your horse through gentle and patient training methods. Use positive reinforcement techniques to help him become more comfortable with being touched.
- **Gradual Desensitization**: Gradual desensitization is also useful for training a horse that is shy about certain parts of its body. Begin by gently touching the area your horse is shy about and gradually build up the intensity and duration of touch over time.
- **Correct Handling Techniques**: Incorrect handling techniques can contribute to a horse's fear or discomfort with certain parts of its body. Make sure you are using proper handling techniques, such as approaching your horse calmly and slowly and avoiding sudden movements.

Pulling Back When Tied

Dealing with a horse that repeatedly pulls back when tied up can be challenging, but it can be overcome with patience and proper training. Horses that develop this issue often pull back extremely violently against the lead rope when tied up and can injure themselves or other horses or people around them. Something about being tied causes them to panic. Here are some steps to safely and calmly work with such a horse:

- **Assess the situation**: Determine if the horse is in immediate danger of injuring themselves or those around them. If so, carefully untie the horse and move them to a safe area.
- **Retrain the horse**: Start by retraining the horse to tie up calmly. Use a sturdy, well-anchored tie-up point and a strong, breakable halter or lead rope. Begin by tying the horse for short periods and gradually increasing the duration as the horse becomes more comfortable. Treats or positive reinforcement may also be helpful in training the horse to stand still.
- **Address the underlying issue**: If the horse is pulling back due to anxiety or fear, it may be helpful to address the underlying issue. Consider working with a trainer or behaviorist who can help identify and address any underlying fears or anxieties that may be contributing to the problem.
- **Be patient and consistent**: Consistency and patience are key when working with a horse that pulls back. Be sure to stay calm and avoid any sudden movements or loud noises that may startle the horse.

Consistently reinforce good behavior and avoid reinforcing any undesirable behavior.

- **Consider alternative methods**: If the horse continues to pull back, consider using alternative methods such as a tie ring, cross ties, or a tie blocker ring. These options allow the horse to move freely but prevent them from breaking away and causing injury.

Working with a horse that repeatedly pulls back when tied up can be challenging and potentially dangerous. It's important to prioritize safety and seek a qualified professional's help if needed.

Won't Stand for Farrier

- **Evaluate the Situation**: Determine the cause of the behavior. The horse may be experiencing pain or discomfort, fear of the farrier or the tools, or simply lack training. The cause of the behavior will dictate what approach to take to remedy the issue. If the horse is in pain, seek medical attention.
- **Desensitization**: Desensitizing your horse to the farrier's tools by using them in non-threatening ways can help reduce fear and anxiety. Pick up your horse's feet yourself several times a week. Have the farrier show you techniques to get your horse to lift his feet. Pick up each foot, hold it for a few minutes, and tap the bottom on the foot to get him used to people touching his feet.

- **Training**: Teaching your horse to stand still during hoof trimming and other farrier work is essential. I have two horses that are not perfect gentlemen for the farrier, but they have both made great strides in the last year through patience and repetition. I lift their feet several times a week. It is also important to have a farrier that is patient but also does not let a horse that likes to push boundaries get away with poor behavior. My farrier and I have worked together to improve these two horses' manners while being trimmed. I do not tie them, I hold the lead rope, loosely, while the farrier does his work. The older horse has issues with pain which contributes to his less than perfect behavior while being trimmed, so I distract him by stroking his lip or offering treats. The farrier uses different positions to trim him that cause him less pain. The younger horse is simply young, curious, and has a very outgoing personality, and is still in training. He has progressed by simply being corrected when he tries to lean on the farrier or move away. Always use positive reinforcement techniques, be firm but not harsh, and first and foremost make sure you understand the reason for the misbehavior so you can choose the correct training techniques.

Rooster getting trimmed as a 2 year old

Won't Load (in a Trailer)

- **Gradual Desensitization**: Start by desensitizing
  your horse to the trailer in a non-threatening way.
  Begin by leading your horse to the trailer and allow
  him to sniff it. Lead him away, then lead him back to
  the trailer several times without asking him to go
  inside. Gradually work up to loading and unloading,
  starting with only one foot in the trailer. When you
  attempt to load him in the trailer fully, walk right
  into the trailer confidently and do not hesitate. If
  your horse stops and will not follow, do not jerk or
  aggressively pull the rope. Remain calm and keep
  gentle but firm pressure on the rope. When your
  horse moves forward immediately release all tension
  on the rope. Release of pressure is a reward for a
  horse. Repeat this until the horse loads into the
  trailer. Remember, if you feel anxious or nervous,
  you'll only make your horse become anxious as well.
  Make yourself "feel" that loading in the trailer is no
  big deal. One useful tip – some horses load easier if
  they can see all the way through the front of the

trailer. Open the front flaps, slats, or windows of the trailer so that he can see daylight on the other side. And, finally, a horse will often load much easier if one of his buddies is already in the trailer. Load the "easy loaders" in the trailer first, and the anxious loader will follow them in much easier than if you try to load him by himself.

- **Patience and Positive Reinforcement**: Again, patience and positive reinforcement are essential when training your horse to load. Rewarding him with treats or praise for stepping onto the trailer can help him learn to load.
- **Use of Tools**: You can also use tools like a lunge line or a helper to encourage the horse into the trailer. But ensure that the tools are used correctly and not too harshly.

Can't Catch Him/Her

Difficulty catching your horse can be frustrating, but there are ways to address it. The first step is to try to identify why your horse is avoiding being caught. It could be that they associate being caught with something unpleasant, like work (yes, some horses are lazier than others just like people), or they may simply not want to leave their herd mates.

To address this problem, start by working on developing a relationship of trust with your horse. Spend time grooming and bonding with your horse on a regular basis without any expectation of riding or work. Make being caught a positive experience for your horse by offering them a treat or some praise when you are successful in catching them.

Another approach is to work on desensitizing your horse to the halter and lead rope. Start by introducing these items in a non-threatening way, such as letting your horse sniff them, and gradually work up to putting them on your horse. Once your horse is comfortable with the halter and lead rope, you can work on leading exercises to build trust and establish clear communication.

"Cold back" Issue

If your horse is exhibiting signs of discomfort or resistance during mounting or riding, such as bucking or pinning their ears back, they may be experiencing cold back. This condition is caused by tension in the muscles of the horse's back, often due to improper warm-up or saddle fit.

To address cold back, start by checking your horse's saddle fit and ensuring that they are warmed up properly before riding. You can also work on exercises to strengthen your horse's back muscles, such as lunging or long-lining. Lunging means using long lead lines, 20 or 30 feet, and flag or lunge whip to encourage the horse to get his feet moving. You need not touch the horse with the flag or whip, simply waiving it near his hindquarters should get him moving. Allow the horse to move further away from you, running bigger and bigger circles, and get him to move from a walk, to a trot, to the lope, and finally into a gallop. Many western riders saddle their horse, and then either lunge the horse or push him around a round pen to warm him up before riding if he has been "cold backed".

If your horse continues to exhibit cold back symptoms despite these efforts, it may be worth consulting with a veterinarian or equine chiropractor to rule out any underlying medical issues.

"Cribbing" Issue

Cribbing is a compulsive behavior in which a horse grasps a solid object with their teeth and sucks in air. This behavior can lead to dental problems, weight loss, and other health issues.

To address cribbing, start by identifying any underlying factors that may be contributing to the behavior, such as boredom or stress. Providing your horse with ample turnout time, toys, and social interaction can help alleviate these factors.

You can also try using a cribbing collar, which is designed to prevent your horse from grasping objects with its teeth. However, it's important to note that cribbing collars should only be used under supervision, as they can be uncomfortable for your horse and may cause other behavioral issues.

"Pica" Issue

Pica is a compulsive behavior in which a horse eats non-food items like dirt or wood. This behavior can lead to digestive problems, colic, and other health issues.

To address pica, start by identifying any underlying factors that may be contributing to the behavior, such as a mineral deficiency. Providing your horse with a balanced diet and access to a mineral block can help alleviate these factors.

You can also try using taste deterrents, such as cayenne pepper or bitter apple, on non-food items to discourage your horse from eating them. However, it's important to note that taste deterrents should only be used under supervision, as they can be ineffective and may cause other behavioral issues.

In conclusion, addressing behavioral issues in horses requires patience, persistence, and a willingness to identify and address underlying factors. By developing a relationship of trust with your horse, addressing any physical or environmental factors that may be contributing to the problem, and using positive reinforcement techniques, you can help your horse overcome problem behaviors and lead a happy, healthy life.

ABUSED HORSES AND THEIR BEHAVIOR

It is heartbreaking to see a horse that has been subjected to abuse and neglect, and even more so to witness their behavioral issues as a result. Fortunately, there are ways to help these horses regain trust and confidence and to correct their behavior. However, it is important to note that sometimes there may not be a complete fix for a horse that has experienced severe abuse. Here are some tips and methods for rehabilitating abused horses:

- **Gaining trust**: The first step in rehabilitating an abused horse is to gain its trust. It is essential to approach them slowly and calmly, avoiding any sudden movements or loud noises that may scare them. Spend time with them, simply sitting in a chair quietly next to their enclosure, and move on to talking to them gently and offering them treats. Approach them only when they are comfortable with your presence and allow them to come to you at their own pace.

- **Patience and consistency**: Patience and consistency are critical when rehabilitating an abused horse. It may require a significant amount of time for the horse to feel comfortable and trusting around humans again. Consistency in your approach, feeding, handling, and care is essential to building their trust and creating a safe environment.

- **Groundwork**: Groundwork is an effective way to train abused horses and gain their trust. Groundwork refers to a variety of exercises that are done on the ground, such as lunging, leading, and desensitization. This type of training allows the horse to understand that you are in control and helps to build a bond of trust between horse and handler.

- **Professional help**: In some cases, an abused horse may require the assistance of a professional trainer or behaviorist. These experts can evaluate the horse's behavior and design a custom training program to help correct their issues. It is essential to choose a trainer with experience working with abused horses and using positive reinforcement methods.

- **Time and patience**: Time and patience are the most important factors in rehabilitating an abused horse. Some horses may require months or even years to fully recover from their past experiences. Remember that these horses need a safe and nurturing environment where they can recover, learn, and grow at their own pace. With time, patience, and a lot of love, many abused horses can make a full recovery and become wonderful companions.

It is important to note that sometimes, despite our best efforts, there may be no complete fix for a horse that has suffered severe abuse. These horses may have deep-rooted issues that cannot be corrected and may require specialized care and understanding throughout their lives. However, with patience, kindness, and a lot of love, we can still provide them with a safe and comfortable life.

IN THIS CHAPTER, we've explored the world of horse behavior, from understanding how horses communicate through body language and vocalizations to recognizing common behavioral issues like aggression, shyness, and cribbing. We've also delved into the factors that can influence a horse's behavior, such as age, experiences, and past abuse.

By paying attention to your horse's body language and vocalizations, you can better understand their needs and avoid potential issues. In addition, by providing appropriate training, handling, and care, you can help prevent or correct behavioral problems in your horse.

In the next chapter, we'll shift our focus to the nutritional care of your horse. We'll explore the basic principles of equine nutrition, including what to feed your horse, how much to feed, and when to feed it. So, keep reading to learn how to ensure your horse gets the proper nutrition they need to thrive.

THE EQUINE GOURMET

> *A clever horse will learn to snatch bites of hay out of your hand or dart into the bucket and grab a mouthful before retreating out of range.*

— IAIN COLEMAN

Proper nutrition is vital for maintaining the health and well-being of horses. A well-fed horse is more likely to be healthy, have a shiny coat, and have the energy needed for daily activities. As a responsible horse owner, it is crucial to understand your horse's nutritional needs and how to provide a balanced and appropriate diet.

In this chapter, we will discuss the essential nutrients horses require, their functions in the body, and how to ensure your horse gets the right amount of each nutrient. We will also delve into different feeding strategies, such as forage-based diets, grain-based diets, and commercial feeds.

By the end of this chapter, you will have a good understanding of the nutritional needs of horses and how to provide a balanced and healthy diet for your equine companion.

FEEDING YOUR HORSE

Feeding your horse is one of the most crucial aspects of horse care. A well-balanced diet not only ensures the overall health and well-being of your horse but also helps maintain their energy levels and performance.

Food and Water

First things first, let's talk about the basics. All your horse needs for good health is good quality hay and access to clean water. Horses need to drink water every day, and the amount they consume depends on various factors like their activity level, diet, and climate. Always provide fresh, clean water in sufficient quantities, especially during hot weather.

Horse Hay vs. Cattle/Other Livestock Hay

Not all hay is created equal, "hay" is not just "hay." While cattle and other livestock can eat lower-quality hay, horses require hay with higher nutritional value. The type of hay your horse needs depends on their age, activity level, and overall health. Grass hay like Timothy, brome, or orchard grass is usually recommended for most horses, while legume hay like alfalfa or clover is more nutrient-rich and is suitable for horses with higher energy needs. Be careful not to feed horses hay that is too rich, as it can lead to laminitis and founder. Laminitis is inflammation and damage of the tissue between the hoof and the underlying coffin bone. In severe cases, it can progress to founder, in which the hoof and the coffin bone are separated and the coffin bone can rotate, leading to severe pain and lameness.

The Delicate Diet of Horses

Horses are delicate creatures that require a proper diet. The ideal diet should consist of hay, which provides fiber and roughage, and concentrated feeds like grains, which supply essential nutrients like protein, fat, and vitamins. It's important to ensure that the horse's diet meets its nutritional requirements, and this varies depending on factors like age, weight, and activity level. Additionally, horses need sufficient minerals and trace elements for optimal health. Again, horses can survive with just quality hay and water, but they will be healthier, live longer, and generally perform better with these supplements.

Grain/Pellets: What's the Deal?

Grain and pellet feeds are popular among horse owners; it's available in various formulas for different types of horses. Many horses thrive on a diet that includes concentrated feed. However, it's important to understand that not all horses require grain. If you do feed your horse grain, make sure to select a feed that is appropriate for their age, weight, and activity level. It's also essential to introduce grains slowly to prevent digestive upsets. I do feed grain to my horses. Not too much, and not every day, but in addition to providing additional nutrients this practice has made my horses very easy to catch. When I whistle they come running, even though I don't give them grain every time I call them in.

Even the chance that they will get it is apparently enough for them! This also gives me the opportunity to give the older horses special supplements for inflamed joints. I halter and tie each of them every time I call them in. They line up and wait patiently to be tied. So, this can be an added benefit of feeding grain.

Treats: A Little Something Extra

Treats can be a great way to bond with your horse, but feeding them in moderation is essential. Treats like apples, carrots, or horse treats that you can buy at any feed store or online can provide a little something extra and add variety to your horse's diet. However, avoid feeding your horse sugary treats like candy or other processed sugar, as they can be harmful to their health.

HOW TO CREATE A BALANCED DIET FOR YOUR HORSE

In this section, we will go over the steps you can take to create a diet tailored to your horse's needs.

What Does Your Horse Need?

The first step in providing proper nutrition for your horse is determining its needs based on age, weight, and work level. For example, a five-year-old horse that works every day will have different caloric and nutritional needs than a sixteen-year-old horse that is only ridden lightly twice a week. It's important to research and consult with a veterinarian or equine nutritionist to determine the appropriate balance of nutrients for your horse. Additionally, you should consider the type of forage and feed available in your area and any health conditions or special needs your horse may have, such as allergies or insulin resistance. By assessing your horse's nutritional needs, you can help ensure they receive the proper diet to maintain good health and performance.

What is Your Horse Eating?

Next, you need to determine what your horse is currently eating. This includes hay, grains, concentrates, supplements, and treats. Knowing what your horse consumes will help you determine what nutrients are lacking in its diet.

The Feeding Guidelines

Once you know what your horse needs and what it's currently eating, you can begin to create a feeding plan that meets its nutritional requirements. Feeding guidelines will differ based on the type of horse and its activity level.

5 Steps to Balance Their Diet

To ensure that your horse's diet is balanced, follow these five steps:

1. Provide clean, fresh water at all times; if you live in a cold climate, have a plan for providing water in winter
2. Provide high-quality hay
3. Add concentrates, if necessary, based on your veterinarian's advice
4. Offer mineral and salt blocks
5. Monitor your horse's body condition score and adjust its diet as needed

Body Condition Score

A body condition score is a numerical rating system used to assess the amount of fat covering a horse's body, which is a key indicator of overall health and nutrition. Monitoring your horse's body condition score regularly is important to ensure they are maintaining a healthy weight and receiving appropriate nutrition.

The body condition score system typically ranges from 1 to 9, with 1 being extremely thin and 9 being extremely obese. A score of 5 is considered ideal for most horses, indicating a healthy balance of fat and muscle covering the horse's body.

To assess your horse's body condition score, look and feel for the amount of fat covering their ribs, backbone, and hips. A horse with a body condition score of 3 or less will have visible ribs and a prominent spine, while a horse with a score of 7 or higher will have excess fat over its ribs and a noticeable crest on its neck.

Based on your horse's body condition score, you may need to adjust their diet by increasing or decreasing their caloric intake or adjusting the balance of nutrients they receive. Working with a veterinarian or equine nutritionist can help ensure your horse's diet is appropriate for its body condition and health needs.

The Schedule

Lastly, creating a feeding schedule that works for your horse and your lifestyle is important. Horses should have access to hay every day, but concentrated feedings can be timed to coincide with work or exercise schedules.

By following these steps, you can create a balanced diet that meets your horse's nutritional needs and keeps it healthy and happy. Remember to monitor your horse's body condition and adjust its diet as needed. A well-fed horse is a happy horse.

IN THIS CHAPTER, you have learned about the essential elements of feeding and creating a balanced diet for your horse. You now understand the importance of providing your horse with the right food and water, the differences between hay for horses and other livestock, and the delicate diet of horses. Additionally, we discussed the benefits and different types of grain and pellets and how to create a balanced diet based on your horse's age, weight, and work level.

In the next chapter, we will delve into grooming and caring for your horses. You will learn about the proper grooming tools, techniques, and routines for your horse's coat, mane, tail, and hooves.

FROM MUCK TO MAJESTY

66 *With a little patience, care, and understanding you can help your horses to be happy, calm, willing to communicate, work with you, be open and trusting of you at all times.*

— HETTY TAPPER

The previous chapter discussed the importance of providing a balanced diet for your equine companions. Now, we're going to shift our focus to another essential aspect of horse care: grooming. Grooming is a crucial part of maintaining your horse's health and well-being and an excellent way to bond with your horse. In this chapter, we'll cover everything you need to know about grooming your horse, from brushing and bathing to mane and tail care.

GROOMING YOUR HORSE

Regular grooming is essential for your horse's overall health and well-being. Not only does it help your horse look good, but it also helps prevent skin infections, keeps your horse's coat shiny and healthy, and promotes bonding between you and your horse.

Why You Should Groom Your Horse Regularly

Grooming is not just about maintaining your horse's appearance. It is also about checking your horse for any signs of illness or injury. During grooming, you can inspect your horse's skin, hooves, eyes, and ears for any problems that may require veterinary attention. Additionally, grooming helps improve blood circulation and reduces the risk of skin irritations, infections, and insect bites.

SUPPLIES NEEDED

It is important to have the right supplies to ensure your horse looks and feels great. Let's go over the supplies you will need to get started.

Basic Grooming Supplies

- **Curry comb**: A curry comb is an essential tool for removing dirt and loose hair from your horse's coat. It is made of rubber or plastic and has small teeth. Use a circular motion to massage your horse's muscles while removing mud, dirt and hair.

- **Hard brush**: A hard brush is used to remove dirt and dust from your horse's coat after using a curry comb. It is made of stiff bristles and is great for getting rid of stubborn dirt.

- **Hoof cleaning brush and hoof pick**: A hoof cleaning brush and pick are used to clean your horse's hooves. Dirt and debris can get trapped in the hoof, so it is important to clean them regularly to avoid any infections or discomfort for your horse.

- **Mane and tail brush**: A mane and tail brush is used to detangle and smooth out your horse's mane and tail. It is made of soft bristles to avoid damaging the hair.

- **Wide-Toothed comb**: A wide-toothed comb is used to detangle any knots or mats in your horse's coat. It is also great for smoothing out your horse's coat after using a hard brush.

- **Soft brush**: A soft brush is used to smooth out your horse's coat after using a hard brush. It is made of soft bristles and is great for removing any remaining dirt or dust.

- **Towel rag**: A towel rag is used to wipe away any sweat or moisture from your horse's coat. It is also great for wiping away any dirt or dust.

Seasonal Grooming Supplies

- **Bot knife**: A bot knife is used to remove bot eggs from your horse's coat. Bot eggs are small yellowish eggs that are laid on your horse's coat by bot flies if you have these where you live.

- **Clippers**: Clippers are used to trim your horse's hair. They are great for trimming your horse's hair around its face, ears, and legs. It is important to choose clippers that are suitable for your horse's coat.
- **Fly spray**: Fly spray is used to keep flies and other insects away from your horse. It is important to choose a fly spray that is safe for your horse and does not cause any skin irritation. Most horses need to be desensitized to fly spray as it can make them nervous at first.
- **Mane-Pulling comb**: A mane-pulling comb is used to thin out your horse's mane. It is great for giving your horse's mane a neat and tidy appearance.
- **Scissors**: Scissors are used to trim your horse's hair. They are great for trimming your horse's hair around its face, ears, and legs. It is important to choose scissors that are suitable for your horse's coat.
- **Sponges**: Sponges are used to clean your horse's coat. They are great for cleaning sensitive areas such as the face and legs.
- **Shedding blade**: A shedding blade is used to remove loose hair from your horse's coat during shedding season. It is important to choose a shedding blade that is suitable for your horse's coat.
- **Sweat scraper**: A sweat scraper is used to remove sweat and moisture from your horse's coat. It is great for after a workout or when your horse gets wet.

How to Groom Your Horse

Before you start grooming, make sure that your horse is secure in a stall or a fenced area. It's essential to ensure that your horse doesn't wander off while you're grooming. If you're grooming a young horse, make sure an adult is present to supervise.

Step 1: Curry Comb

Use a curry comb to break up any dirt, mud, or debris from your horse's coat. Use a circular motion and apply gentle pressure while currying. Make sure to avoid sensitive areas like the face, legs, and stomach or any scrapes or cuts.

Step 2: Hard Brush

Next, use a hard brush to remove dirt and debris from your horse's coat. Use a flicking motion to brush the hair in the direction of the coat. Start from the top of the horse and work your way down. Make sure to brush the horse's sides, back, and legs.

Step 3: Soft Brush

Once you've removed most of the dirt, use a soft brush to remove any remaining dust and dirt. The soft brush is gentler and helps smooth out the coat. Use a flicking motion to brush the horse's coat in the direction of hair growth. This is an excellent time to focus on sensitive areas like the horse's face, ears, and legs.

Step 4: Clean the Hooves

Use a hoof pick to remove dirt and debris from your horse's hooves. Make sure to remove any rocks, mud, or manure stuck in the hooves. Regular hoof cleaning helps prevent infections and lameness. I always do a quick check for rocks in my horse's hooves before I ride.

Step 5: Mane and Tail

Finally, brush the horse's mane and tail using a hard brush or a mane brush. Start from the bottom of the hair and work your way up, gently detangling any knots as you go.

You don't need to do this every day. If it rains, and your horse gets muddy, you don't have to rush out to the pasture and clean him up immediately. If your horse is prone to skin issues, you probably need to groom him more often, but you don't to go overboard if you have a generally healthy horse.

IN THIS CHAPTER, we discussed the essential grooming supplies needed to keep your horse healthy and happy. We covered basic supplies such as the curry comb, hard brush, and soft brush, as well as seasonal supplies such as clippers and fly spray. It is important to have these supplies on hand to ensure proper grooming of your horse and to build a strong bond between you and your equine friend.

In the next chapter, we will discuss how to protect your horse from the elements. Weather can be unpredictable and harsh, but with the right tools and knowledge, you can keep your horse safe and comfortable. We will cover topics such as shelter, blankets, and proper nutrition. Continue reading to learn more about how to protect your horse from the severity of weather elements and ensure their overall well-being.

WEATHER WARRIORS

WHOSE WOODS THESE ARE I THINK I KNOW.

His house is in the village, though;

He will not see me stopping here

To watch his woods fill up with snow.

My little horse must think it queer

To stop without a farmhouse near

Between the woods and frozen lake

The darkest evening of the year.

He gives his harness bells a shake

To ask if there is some mistake.

The only other sound's the sweep

Of easy wind and downy flake.

The woods are lovely, dark, and deep,

But I have promises to keep,

And miles to go before I sleep,

And miles to go before I sleep.

— ROBERT FROST

In this chapter, we will discuss various ways to protect your horse from the harshness of weather, including shelter, blankets, and proper nutrition. By implementing these strategies, you can ensure your horse stays comfortable, healthy, and happy. So, let's dive in and learn how to protect your equine friend from the severity of weather elements.

Protecting your horse from harsh weather elements is essential to ensure its health and well-being. In this chapter, we will discuss how to protect your horse from both hot and cold weather conditions. We will also explore different breeds' tolerances to heat and cold and how to manage your horse's shelter, feeding, and water requirements.

HORSES AND HEAT

During hot weather, horses can be at risk of overheating, which can lead to heat exhaustion or heat stroke. Therefore, it's crucial to know how to keep your horse cool during the hot summer months. Sweating is a natural cooling mechanism, and it's essential to keep your horse well-hydrated. You can also use techniques such as cold hosing, applying wet towels, or using fans to help cool down your horse. Acclimating your horse to the heat is also crucial to help them cope with the heat stress. Providing areas of shade, either from trees or manmade structures is also required.

Warm Weather Infectious Diseases

Horses are at risk of contracting diseases such as the West Nile Virus, Eastern Equine Encephalitis, and Equine Herpesvirus during hot weather. Therefore, it's important to be aware of these diseases and take the necessary precautions to protect your horse.

HORSES AND COLD

Healthy horses can survive in cold temperatures if they have access to good hay and clean, unfrozen water. Different breeds have different tolerances to cold, and it's essential to know your horse's breed and its specific needs. Temperatures can reach -30 degrees Fahrenheit, and even -50 degrees with the wind chill where I live. I have American Quarter Horses and American Paint Horses, and they do just fine. A horse's coat provides insulation against the cold, and snow accumulation on their backs indicates that their coat is working correctly. Proper management of shelter, feeding, and water requirements is essential during the cold winter months. While these "cold weather" horses are made to withstand the cold, in extreme temperatures you need to provide plenty of food and wind breaks. The process of digesting food helps keep a horse warm. If a horse somehow gets wet and is out in extreme cold, he will also require intervention from you. You need to get him dried off as he will not be able to regulate his body temperature if he is wet in extreme cold.

Thermoregulation in Cold Weather

A horse's coat protects them from the cold, and it's essential to keep it in good condition. Proper grooming during the winter is important to keep their coat healthy and prevent matting, but do not think that you have to brush snow off of a horse. The snow will actually help create even more of an insulation and hold the horse's body heat in. It's also important to provide shelter during the winter months to protect your horse from the wind and precipitation.

Management of Horses in Cold Weather

Proper feeding is crucial during the cold winter months. Horses have different energy requirements during the winter, and it's important to adjust their feed accordingly. It's also important to provide clean, unfrozen water and salt to meet their needs. Keeping water unfrozen in cold climates can be a challenge, and different options can be explored, such as heated water buckets. Blanketing may be necessary for older horses or horses that are not as healthy. However, generally, horses do not need blankets, and it's essential to understand when your horse needs one. Blankets that get stuck to a horse for whatever reason, especially in extreme cold, can do more harm than good. I personally never blanket my horses unless one of them has a health issue that prevents him from properly regulating his body temperature naturally. Some horse lovers ALWAYS blanket their horses, and this topic is hotly debated so you will have to research the pros and cons and make your own informed choice.

IN CONCLUSION, protecting your horse from harsh weather elements is crucial to ensure its health and well-being. Different breeds have different tolerances to heat and cold, and it's important to know your horse's specific needs. Proper management of shelter, feeding, and water requirements is also essential during the different seasons.

APPENDIX: COLORS AND MARKINGS OF YOUR HORSE

FIVE BASIC HORSE COAT COLORS

- **Bay**: A bay horse has a reddish-brown body with black points (mane, tail, and lower legs).
- **Black**: A black horse has a black body, mane, and tail.
- **Brown**: A brown horse can range in color from light to dark brown and has black points.
- **Chestnut**: A chestnut horse has a reddish-brown body and a mane and tail of the same or lighter color.
- **Gray**: A gray horse is any horse of white or gray color, with black skin.
- **White**: A white horse is born white and has pink skin and white hair. It can have blue or brown eyes.

APPENDIX: COLORS AND MARKINGS OF YOUR HORSE

FIVE MAJOR VARIATIONS TO COAT COLORS

- **Dun**: A dun horse has a yellowish-brown body with a black mane and tail. It also has a dorsal stripe down its back.
- **Gray**: A gray horse has black skin and a white or gray coat that becomes lighter with age.
- **Palomino**: A palomino horse has a golden coat with a white or cream mane and tail.
- **Pinto**: A pinto horse has a coat pattern of large patches of white and another color, such as black or brown.
- **Roan**: A roan horse has a coat that is mostly white hair mixed with colored hairs, giving it a speckled appearance.

VARIATIONS OF COLOR PATTERNS OF HEAD AND POINTS

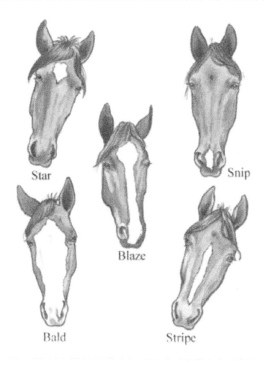

- **Star**: A white marking on a horse's forehead.
- **Snip**: A small white marking on a horse's muzzle.
- **Stripe**: A white marking down a horse's face.
- **Blaze**: A large white marking down a horse's face.
- **Bald face**: A horse with extensive white markings on its face, often covering both eyes.
- **Star, stripe, and snip**: A combination of these markings on a horse's face.
- **Star and stripe**: A combination of a star and stripe on a horse's face.

EYES AND FACE

- **Mealy mouthed**: A horse with light-colored lips and nostrils.

FEET AND LEGS

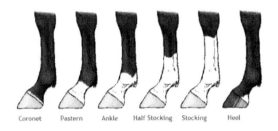

Coronet   Pastern   Ankle   Half Stocking   Stocking   Heel

- **Coronet**: A white marking at the coronet band at the top of a horse's hoof.
- **Pastern**: White markings on a horse's pasterns (the area above the hoof).
- **Ankle:** White markings on a horse's ankles.
- **Half-Stocking**: White marking that covers the bottom half of a horse's leg.
- **Full Stocking**: White marking that covers the entire leg.
- **Outside heel white extending**: A white marking that extends down the outside of a horse's hoof.
- **Outside heel**: A white marking on the outside of a horse's hoof.
- **Inside heel**: A white marking on the inside of a horse's hoof.

MANE AND TAIL

- **Flex and Flaxen**: Flex refers to a mane that falls to one side, while flaxen refers to a mane or tail that is pale yellow in color.
- **Silver**: This describes a coat color that appears to have a silver sheen or metallic shine.
- **True**: This term is used to describe a horse whose coat color is not diluted by any other color genes, resulting in a solid, non-patterned coat color.
- **Rat-tailed**: This term is used to describe a horse whose tail is thin and sparse, giving the appearance of a rat's tail.
- **Broom-tailed or Band-tailed**: These terms describe the texture of a horse's tail. A broom-tailed horse has a thick, full tail, while a band-tailed horse has a tail that is thin and banded.

ADDITIONAL DESCRIPTIVE TERMS

- **Black points**: This term refers to a horse whose ears, mane, and tail are black in color, regardless of the color of the rest of its coat.
- **Calico**: This term is used to describe a horse whose coat has three or more distinct colors in large patches.
- **Cross**: A horse with a white marking that runs across the withers is said to have a cross.
- **Dappled**: This term describes a horse whose coat has circular, slightly darker spots on a lighter

background.

- **Dark**: This term simply refers to a horse with a coat color that is darker than usual for its breed.
- **Flea-bitten**: This term is used to describe a coat color that appears white or gray, but has small reddish-brown speckles throughout.

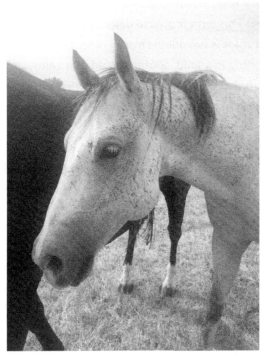

Bugzy is a good example of Flea-bitten gray coloring

- **Golden**: This term is used to describe a horse whose coat color is a rich, deep shade of golden brown.
- **Light**: This term is used to describe a horse whose coat color is lighter than usual for its breed.

- **Line back**: A horse with a dark stripe running along its spine is said to have a line back.
- **Patched**: This term is used to describe a horse whose coat has irregular patches of color.
- **Piebald**: This term describes a horse whose coat is black and white in large, irregular patches.
- **Pure**: This term is used to describe a horse whose coat color is uniform and free of any markings or patterns.
- **Ratty**: This term is used to describe a horse whose coat is rough and unkempt.
- **Ray**: This term is used to describe a horse whose coat has a distinct, straight line of hair running down the middle of its face.
- **Red-speckled**: This term is used to describe a coat color that appears white or gray, but has small red speckles throughout.
- **Skewbald**: This term describes a horse whose coat is white and any other color except black.
- **Smoky**: This term is used to describe a horse whose coat appears to have a smoky or hazy quality.
- **Striped**: This term is used to describe a horse whose coat has narrow stripes of a different color running down its body.
- **Spotted**: This term is used to describe a horse whose coat has large, round spots of a different color.
- **Toasted**: This term is used to describe a coat color that appears to have a warm, toasted quality.
- **Zebra**: This term is used to describe a horse whose coat has stripes like that of a zebra.

CONCLUSION

I hope this book has inspired you to continue on your journey with your equine companion, always prioritizing their health, safety, and well-being. Keep learning, exploring, and pushing your boundaries to deepen your connection with your horse.

This book delves into the fascinating world of equine companionship. Throughout its pages, readers learn the importance of understanding horses' natural behavior, needs, and preferences to establish a deep and meaningful connection.

The key takeaway of this book is that communication, respect, and trust are essential to building a strong bond with your horse. By taking the time to listen to your horse, understanding their body language, and meeting their physical and emotional needs, you can create a relationship based on mutual understanding and respect.

One inspiring success story that illustrates this is that of a young girl who rescued a traumatized horse and transformed him into a confident and happy companion through patience, kindness, and understanding. This story is a testament to the power of patience, empathy, and dedication in developing a strong bond with your horse.

Thank you for choosing to read this book, and I wish you all the best on your journey with your equine companion. If you found this book informative, helpful, and enjoyable, please leave a review to help other readers discover the joys of horses.

Reviews from readers like you support independent writers!

BIBLIOGRAPHY

Abel, C. (2021, October 30). *Pros & Cons Of Owning A Horse: From An Actual Horse Owner*. Equine Helper. https://equinehelper.com/pros-cons-of-owning-a-horse/

Abel, C. (2022, April 1). *21 Common Horse Colors, Markings, & Patterns With Pictures*. Equine Helper. https://equinehelper.com/21-common-horse-colors/

All Horse Breeds - Complete List of Horse Profiles. (n.d.). DiscoverTheHorse. https://www.discoverthehorse.com/horse-breeds/profiles

Amanda Uechi Ronan. (2016, March 21). *What The Muck Is That? Eponychium*. HORSE NATION. https://www.horsenation.com/2016/03/21/what-the-muck-is-that-eponychium/

Avis-Riordan, K. (2017, November 3). *Horses can read human body language, new research finds*. Country Living. https://www.countryliving.com/uk/wildlife/countryside/news/a2797/horse-read-human-body-language/

B, J. (2015, April 20). *Myth: Horses Require Higher Quality Hay Than Cattle*. SUCCEED Equine. https://www.succeed-equine.com/succeed-blog/2015/04/20/monday-myth-horses-require-higher-quality-hay-than-cattle/

Baltimore Sun. (1997). *Monty Roberts: learning the language of horses*. Baltimore Sun. https://www.baltimoresun.com/news/bs-xpm-1997-08-10-1997222022-story.html

Bealing, J. (n.d.). *Horses can read our body language, even when they don't know us*. The University of Sussex. https://www.sussex.ac.uk/broadcast/read/42417

Bonnette, E. (2021, February 10). *5 steps to balancing your horse's diet*. Hubbard Feeds. https://www.hubbardfeeds.com/blog/5-steps-balancing-your-horses-diet

Burattini, B., Fenner, K., Anzulewicz, A., Romness, N., McKenzie, J., Wilson, B., & McGreevy, P. (2020). Age-Related Changes in the Behaviour of Domestic Horses as Reported by Owners. *Animals : An Open Access Journal from MDPI, 10(12)*. https://doi.org/10.3390/ani10122321

Camaro, F., & Coleman, S. (2017). *Blanketing Horses: Do's and Don'ts*. Uky.edu.

https://afs.ca.uky.edu/content/blanketing-horses-do%E2%80%99s-and-don%E2%80%99ts

Can't Afford a Horse? 5 Ways to Stay Involved. (n.d.). Www.equinavia.com. https://www.equinavia.com/get-involved-with-horses

Carmella. (2020, December 14). *What Horse Hooves Are Made Of: Complete Guide.* Equine Helper. https://equinehelper.com/what-horse-hooves-are-made-of/

Coleman, S. E. (2014, July 25). *5 Best Types of Fencing for Horse Farms.* Horse Illustrated Magazine. https://www.horseillustrated.com/5-best-types-of-horse-fencing

Cowboy Magic. (2014, June 2). *20 Horse Quotes.* Cowboy Magic. https://cowboymagic.com/20-horse-quotes-cowboy-magic/

Curiosity and Exploration. (n.d.). Enriching Equines. https://enrichingequines.com/exploration-and-novelty/

Dance, A. (2022, May 19). *When Did Humans Domesticate the Horse?* Smithsonian Magazine. https://www.smithsonianmag.com/science-nature/when-did-humans-domesticate-the-horse-180980097/

Daniel. (2021, April 24). *How Much Space Does a Horse Need?* Animal Food Planet. https://www.animalfoodplanet.com/how-much-space-does-a-horse-need/

Darrean, G. (n.d.). *Horse Behavior: What It Means To Be A Prey Animal.* Happy Horse Training. http://www.happy-horse-training.com/horse-behavior.html

Davies, N. (2014, September 27). *The horse as a "prey" animal.* Horsetalk.co.nz. https://www.horsetalk.co.nz/2014/09/28/horse-prey-animal/

Deep Hollow Ranch. (2021a, June 6). *What Is a Baby Horse Called? (9 Facts About Baby Horse).* Deep Hollow Ranch. https://www.deephollowranch.com/what-is-a-baby-horse-called/

Deep Hollow Ranch. (2021b, August 14). *8 Horse Sounds & The Meaning (Videos Including!).* Deep Hollow Ranch. https://www.deephollowranch.com/horse-noises/

Does letting fields for horses create an agricultural tenancy? (n.d.). Shepwedd.com. https://shepwedd.com/knowledge/does-letting-fields-horses-create-agricultural-tenancy

Eating of Non-food Items in Horses. (2011, November 3). Www.petmd.com. https://www.petmd.com/horse/conditions/behavioral/c_hr_coprophagy

Editorial, C. (2018, May 10). *Horse Toys: How to Keep Your Horse Mentally Stimulated.* BeChewy. https://be.chewy.com/horse-toys-keep-your-horse-mentally-stimulated/

11 Fun Ideas To Mentally Stimulate Your Horse And Prevent Boredom. (2021,

November 6). Ruffle Snuffle - Life with Pets. https://www.rufflesnuffle.-co.uk/11-fun-ideas-to-mentally-stimulate-your-horse-and-prevent-boredom/

Equi-Spa. (2020, June 22). *Answering Questions About Horseshoes: Everything You Wanted to Know.* Equi-Spa. https://equispa.com/2020/06/22/do-horse-shoes-hurt-my-horse-and-other-questions-about-horseshoes-youve-always-wanted-to-ask/

Equinews. (2011, March 10). *Is Cow Hay the Same as Horse Hay?* Kentucky Equine Research. https://ker.com/equinews/cow-hay-horse-hay/

Equus. (2014, September 15). *10 facts about horses and hot weather.* Equus Magazine. https://equusmagazine.com/horse-care/10-facts-horses-hot-weather-25168/

Eva. (2020, April 12). *The realities of owning a horse: the good, the ugly and the dirty truth.* My Life Is Better with Horses. https://www.mylifeisbetter-withhorses.com/the-realities-of-owning-a-horse-the-good-the-ugly-and-the-dirty-truth/

Farriers Registration Council : What is a Farrier? (n.d.). Www.farrier-Reg.gov.uk. https://www.farrier-reg.gov.uk/what-is-a-farrier

Fast Horses: What Makes Them Run Faster Than The Others. (2022, August 30). Horseracingsense. https://horseracingsense.com/fast-horses-makes-run-faster/

Fought, E. (2022, July 21). *Pros & Cons Of Horse Ownership.* COWGIRL Maga-zine. https://cowgirlmagazine.com/pros-cons-of-horse-ownership/

4-H Horse Program. (n.d.). Ext.vt.edu. https://ext.vt.edu/4h-youth/horse.html

G, N. (2022, August 14). *29 Horse Coat Color Variations (Beginner Photo Guide).* Horse Rookie. https://horserookie.com/horse-colors/

Gerkensmeyer, R. (2021, April 16). *7 Common Horse Sounds and What They Mean (With Audio).* Pet Keen. https://petkeen.com/common-horse-sounds/

Good Reads. (n.d.-a). *A quote by Ralph Waldo Emerson.* Www.goodreads.com. https://www.goodreads.com/quotes/19888-riding-a-horse-is-not-a-gentle-hobby-to-be

Good Reads. (n.d.-b). *Showing all quotes that contain "horse".* Www.goodreads.-com. https://www.goodreads.com/quotes/search?commit=Search&page=3&q=horse&utf8=%E2%9C%93

Good Reads. (n.d.-c). *Walter Farley Quotes (Author of The Black Stallion).* Www.-goodreads.com. https://www.goodreads.com/author/quotes/16628.Walter_Farley

Health Fitness Revolution. (2017, October 26). *Top 10 Health Benefits of*

Owning a Horse. Health Fitness Revolution. https://www.healthfitnessrevolution.com/top-10-health-benefits-owning-horse/

Heart of Horsemanship. (n.d.). *Horses are prey animals,we are preditors.* Mysite. https://www.theheartofhorsemanship.net/horses-are-prey-animals-we-are-pred

Horse anatomy - diagrams of horse body parts. (n.d.). Www.equishop.com. https://www.equishop.com/en/blog/horse-anatomy-body-parts-muscles-skeleton-n299

Horse grooming 101: A guide for beginners. (2020, September 8). Horse & Country TV. https://horseandcountry.tv/en-us/horse-grooming-101-a-guide-for-beginners/

Horse Hoof Cross Section. (n.d.). Cf. https://cf.ltkcdn.net/horses/files/3511-horsehoofxsection.pdf

Horse Temperament: What Is The Best For A Beginner Rider? (2021, July 23). Horseracingsense. https://horseracingsense.com/horse-temperament-best-for-beginner-rider

Horses Health. (2020, January 20). *Determining the Age of Horses by Their Teeth.* Horses.extension.org. https://horses.extension.org/determining-the-age-of-horses-by-their-teeth/

Hyde, J. (2019, October 17). *10 Things That Make Horse & Human Relationships.* Pet Urns & Pet Cremation Services. https://agapepetservices.com/make-horse-human-relationships-unique/

The importance of the hoof and its health (no hoof, no horse). (2018, January 2). Finish Line® Horse Products, Inc. https://www.finishlinehorse.com/2018/01/the-importance-of-the-hoof-and-its-health-no-hoof-no-horse/

Job, D. (2020, October 15). *The Best 24/7 Horse Fencing Options for Your Farm.* Systemequine.com. https://systemequine.com/blog/the-best-fencing-options-for-your-outdoor-horse-farm/

Johnson, D. (n.d.). *Behavioral Problems in Horses.* Horsehints.org. http://horsehints.org/BehavioralProblems.htm

Jones, J. (2020). *Horse-human cooperation is a neurobiological miracle.* Aeon. https://aeon.co/essays/horse-human-cooperation-is-a-neurobiological-miracle

KBIS. (2022, April 14). *Ten things to consider when buying a new horse.* KBIS. https://www.kbis.co.uk/advice/10-things-to-consider-when-buying-a-new-horse/

King, A.-J. (2022, November 3). *How to Read a Horse's Body Language.* Www.petmd.com. https://www.petmd.com/horse/how-read-horses-body-language

Kip. (2019, February 1). *"Ode to the Horse" by Ronald Duncan*. Kipmistral. https://www.kipmistral.com/ode-to-the-horse-by-ronald-duncan/

Lauren Cassani Davis. (2016, February 29). *Study: Domestic Horses Can Detect Negative Emotion in Human Facial Expressions*. The Atlantic. https://www.theatlantic.com/science/archive/2016/02/how-horses-read-human-emotions/471264/

Leasing my land for someone to keep horses on? (n.d.). The Horse Forum. https://www.horseforum.com/threads/leasing-my-land-for-someone-to-keep-horses-on.133036/

Lee, A. (2019, November 27). *List of 40 Horse Breeds w/ Pictures, Description & Registry Links*. Helpful Horse Hints. https://www.helpfulhorsehints.-com/horse-breeds/

Lesté-Lasserre, MA, C. (2020, January 2). *Researcher: Horses Are "Emotional Sponges."* The Horse. https://thehorse.com/182990/researcher-horses-are-emotional-sponges/

Main Types of Horse Personalities. (2018, February 7). Horse Network. https://horsenetwork.com/2018/02/main-types-horse-personalities/

Male Or Female Horse: The Pros And Cons Of Each. (2022, May 17). Horserac-ingsense. https://horseracingsense.com/male-or-female-horse-pros-cons/

Maria. (2019, December 11). *5 Stages of a Horse's Life Cycle*. Horses and Us. https://www.horsesandus.com/5-stages-of-a-horses-life-cycle/

McCart, R. (2020, May 21). *Read This Before You Buy Your First Horse*. The Horse. https://thehorse.com/135881/read-this-before-you-buy-your-first-horse/

McClure, R. (n.d.). *Functional Anatomy of the Horse Foot*. Extension.mis-souri.edu. https://extension.missouri.edu/publications/g2740

Merkies, K., & Franzin, O. (2021). *Enhanced Understanding of Horse–Human Interactions to Optimize Welfare*. Animals, 11(5), 1347. https://doi.org/10.3390/ani11051347

MNH. (2020, November 17). *What Join Up means*. Natural-Horsemanship. https://www.naturalhorsemanshipindia.com/single-post/what-join-up-means

Moody, D. (2017, January 10). *What to Do When You Can't Afford a Horse*. Horse Network. https://horsenetwork.com/2017/01/cant-afford-horse/

Murphy, J., Hall, C., & Arkins, S. (2009). What Horses and Humans See: A Comparative Review. *International Journal of Zoology, 2009, 1.* https://www.academia.edu/27508200/What_Horses_and_Human-s_See_A_Comparative_Review

NIdirect. (2015, November 20). *Horses: the need for a suitable environment*.

Nidirect.   https://www.nidirect.gov.uk/articles/horses-need-suitable-environment

Nidirect. (2015, November 20). *Welfare of horses: the need for a suitable diet.* Nidirect. https://www.nidirect.gov.uk/articles/welfare-horses-need-suitable-diet

Observing Wild Horse Behavior. (2010). https://www.nps.gov/calo/learn/nature/upload/2006-Observing-Wild-Horse-Behavior.pdf

1.2 Horse Behaviour: Wild vs. Stabled. (n.d.). Thehorseportal.ca. https://thehorseportal.ca/lesson/1-2-horse-behaviour-wild-vs-stabled-4/

Owen, J. (2005, March 17). *Horse Evolution Followed Twisty Trail, Study Says.* Animals.   https://www.nationalgeographic.com/animals/article/horse-evolution-news-animals

Parts of a Horse: Useful Horse Anatomy with Pictures. (2018). 7esl.com. https://7esl.com/parts-of-a-horse/

Paulick Race Staff. (2019, June 12). *Ever Wonder Why Racehorses Are So Fast? Tufts University Explains.* Paulickreport.com. https://paulickreport.com/horse-care-category/ever-wonder-why-racehorses-are-so-fast-tufts-university-explains/

PhD, J. L. J. (2016, January 29). *How your horse's vision differs from yours.* Equus Magazine. https://equusmagazine.com/behavior/eye-eye-31022/

Reed, J. (n.d.). *5 Ways Horses Increase Happiness.* Www.acreagelife.com. https://www.acreagelife.com/hobby-farming/5-ways-horses-increase-happiness

Royal Horse. (n.d.). *What do horses eat?* Royal Horse. https://www.royal-horse.com/advice/what-do-horses-eat/

S, C. (2019). *Life Cycle of a Horse: Lesson for Kids.* Study.com. https://study.com/academy/lesson/life-cycle-of-a-horse-lesson-for-kids.html

Sarah. (2020, July 7). *Pica in Horses- The desire to eat unusual substances.* Ranvet. https://www.ranvet.com.au/pica-in-horses/

Selecting Hay for Your Horse: Separating the Facts from the Fiction. (n.d.). Equine.ca.uky.edu. https://equine.ca.uky.edu/content/selecting-hay-your-horse-separating-facts-fiction

Smith Thomas, H. (2019, January 30). *The Hardy Horse: How Horses Handle Winter.* The Horse. https://thehorse.com/150475/the-hardy-horse-how-horses-handle-winter/

SPANA. (2018, August 28). *What Do Horses Eat?* SPANA. https://spana.org/blog/what-do-horses-eat/

Spruce Official. (n.d.). *8 Tips That Can Help You Form A Bond With Your Horse.* The Spruce Pets. https://www.thesprucepets.com/how-do-i-bond-with-my-horse-1886822

Spruce Official. (2019). *Learn the Basics of Training Your Horse.* The Spruce Pets. https://www.thesprucepets.com/training-your-horse-1886992

Standlee Forage. (2021, October 6). *What is the Difference Between Hay, Straw and Premium Forage?* Standlee Premium Products. https://www.standleeforage.com/standlee-barn-bulletin/difference-between-hay-straw-and-premium-forage/

Tallis, N. (2012, May 22). *Horses and human history.* The British Museum. https://www.britishmuseum.org/blog/horses-and-human-history

Tips on Buying Your First Horse. (2012). Rutgers.edu. https://esc.rutgers.edu/fact_sheet/tips-on-buying-your-first-horse/

Trösch, Cuzol, Parias, Calandreau, Nowak, & Lansade. (2019). *Horses Categorize Human Emotions Cross-Modally Based on Facial Expression and Non-Verbal Vocalizations. Animals, 9(11), 862.* https://doi.org/10.3390/ani9110862

24 Ways To Increase Your Horse Property Income. (2021, June 24). Horse Journals. https://www.horsejournals.com/acreages-stables/barns-stables/24-ways-increase-your-horse-property-income

University, U. S. (n.d.). *Foal Hoof Care: When and How Often to Trim?* Extension.usu.edu. https://extension.usu.edu/equine/research/foal-hoof-care

Vandenborre, K. (2019, July 5). *Nurturing the natural curiosity of your horse.* Horsefulness Training. https://horsefulnesstraining.com/nurturing-the-natural-curiosity-of-your-horse/

Wallace, H. (2021, July 10). *Experiencing The Movement 2021 with Monty Roberts.* Horse Illustrated Magazine. https://www.horseillustrated.com/the-movement-2021-monty-roberts

What do horses eat? (2023). Study.com. https://study.com/academy/lesson/what-do-horses-eat-lesson-for-kids.html

What you need to know about owning your first horse. (2021, April 18). Finish Line® Horse Products, Inc. https://www.finishlinehorse.com/2021/04/what-you-need-to-know-about-owning-your-first-horse/

Williams, C. A. (2019). *The Basics of Equine Behavior.* Rutgers.edu. https://esc.rutgers.edu/fact_sheet/the-basics-of-equine-behavior/

Williams, J. (2013, January 30). *Horse Body Language: How To Read It And Understand It.* Equus Magazine. https://equusmagazine.com/behavior/horse-body-language/

Wise Sayings. (n.d.). *Horses Sayings and Horses Quotes.* Www.wisesayings.com. https://www.wisesayings.com/horses-quotes/

World Horse Welfare. (n.d.). *Stabling a horse.* Www.worldhorsewelfare.org. https://www.worldhorsewelfare.org/advice/management/stabling

IMAGE REFERENCES

Fairy Fingers. (n.d.). HORSE NATION. http://www.horsenation.com

Leg Faults. (n.d.). Www.horseloverz.com. http://horselovers.com

Leg Markings. (n.d.). My Corral. http://mycorral.weebly.com/leg-markings.html

Lemons, S. (2012, July 18). *NC Horse Blog: White Facial Markings Can be Used for Equine Identification.* NC Horse Blog. http://nchorse.blogspot.com/2012/07/white-facial-markings-can-be-used-for.html